Over Our Hearts

A mother's journey learning to listen in.

*Your light shines
so bright it can't help
but glow! love you! Shana*

P. 141

by Shana Lynn Schmidt

OVER OUR HEARTS;
A MOTHER'S JOURNEY LEARNING TO LISTEN IN
Copyright © 2019 by Shana Lynn Schmidt

First Edition, 2019
ISBN 978-1-08191-699-2

Indie Published by Shana Lynn Schmidt
Cover design: Jace Schmidt
Photos: Xpressions by Kim

To Theo.

The best surprise ever.

chapter | *Contents*

introduction | *Kaete & Erick*

It was near the end of the month, and I still had not had my period. This was common for me – I was very active and had not had consistent periods in the past. But something was different this time. I knew in my heart that my biggest fear had become a reality. Something I had joked about as a naive middle schooler was now happening to me. I told my boyfriend Erick I had a feeling I was pregnant. In disbelief, we agreed to tell no one and just wait to see if what my heart already knew was really true.

After a week of "waiting it out," I decided I needed to tell my parents. This was too much to hold in my heart any more. I could no longer keep such a huge secret from the most important people in my life. After being infatuated with babies and pregnancy since I was a toddler, I knew I needed to begin prenatal vitamins and receive all the necessary medical attention, to make sure that if there *was* a tiny life inside me, it would grow to be a healthy child. After all, it did not feel fair to make a small, defenseless child pay the price for me being too scared to share what I thought might be going on in my body.

I told Erick I was going to tell my parents and we agreed it was the best thing to do. Although terrified, we were willing to accept the consequences. It took me quite a while to build the confidence to finally tell them. I wanted to tell them in the perfect way, at the perfect time. As it turns out, that is not possible when a 14-year-old is announcing her own pregnancy.

Finally, one night as I lay in bed, I forced myself to yell "Mom!" I could hear her feet hit the floor and the bedroom door open. Numbness took over my body. I burst into tears the second I saw her in my doorway. Confused, she held me in her arms until I regained enough breath to tell her what I suspected. We sat together in my bed with tears streaming down both of our faces. What felt like hours was only 10 minutes.

Before I told my parents, I had imagined all the possible outcomes. These included: they force me to break up with Erick; they stop loving me the same; they are embarrassed by me; they stop talking to me; they kick me out; they lose business because of me. Society had taught me teen parents were not wanted by anyone. I hoped my parents would find forgiveness in their hearts, but I was prepared for the worst.

None of this could have prepared me for my parents' response. There was never a day throughout my pregnancy that they allowed me or Erick to feel like they did not love or respect us. I continued to make up stories in my head about how embarrassing I was and how they probably did not want a pregnant daughter, but I was always reassured of their unconditional love.

Telling Erick's parents took a little bit longer. He had no idea how they would react and was scared of the thought of disappointing them. Three weeks after I broke the news to my parents, Erick gathered enough courage to tell his. They, too, wanted nothing but the best for us both. Just like my parents, they continued to show unconditional love to us every day and never made us feel as if our child was anything less than a blessing.

The first few weeks after telling my parents was absolutely horrible. I am not going sugar-coat it. I felt like a failure, completely unlovable, and like my life was over. I walked around faking smiles, but inside I was completely numb. I could no longer cry or feel happiness or sadness, just numbness.

Erick describes this time as being very lonely. He felt the same as I did – empty and emotionless – as we tried to live our lives as if nothing was different. But we knew *everything* was different. To this day, when I think back on those first couple weeks, I still feel as if I cannot breathe and I can feel the numbness all over again. I blocked a lot of that time out and cannot remember many details of those first few weeks due to my feeling of hopelessness.

Today, I could not be happier with my life. I have a beautiful, healthy little boy. I have an amazing and supportive boyfriend. I have a house for our little family to live in. I graduated from high school with honors and get to attend college for free with scholarships I received. What I thought was a complete disaster that would lead me in a different direction than I had hoped turned into the absolute best thing to happen to me.

I have never felt more love than I do today from family, friends, and community members. My son Theo is the biggest blessing in my life and has taught me perseverance, strength, and overall how to be the best me I can possibly be. He did not cause me to give up my dreams – he gave me a reason to strive harder to reach them. I pushed myself every single day at school and at home to achieve everything I wanted and more, all for my son and family, to give him the best possible future.

Erick and Theo have become the best parts of my life and I am thankful for them every day. To be where I am today was nothing I could have ever possibly imagined the day I found out I was pregnant. I could not have done any of it without the support and love from everyone around me.

After facing one of the greatest challenges in our lives, we have learned that you can achieve anything you set your mind to. With love, support, and listening to what matters to you, no hurdle is too high to keep you from reaching your dreams. Nothing is impossible.

To keep up with us go to YouTube and subscribe:
KElittleT

one | *Surprises*

Choose wisely the words you say to your children, to others, to yourself. Words have a way of becoming truths we believe about ourselves. And what we believe, we become. L.R. Knost

It was past 11 p.m. when she called me. *"Mom? Mom? MOM?"* Drifting to sleep feels like a whisper from life, reminding me of another day passed and a job well done. The sounds around me fade into questions of *Am I dreaming, or is this real life?*

In the quiet dark of our bedroom, I was uncertain if I heard my name and rolled over quietly asking my husband, *"Is Kaete calling for me?"* He verified she was. I stumbled from bed, feeling simultaneously irritated about missing sleep and grateful for the call to join my baby girl in the dark.

Typically, this type of call comes an hour or two after she's been tucked into bed and goodnights have been shared, but only when something is weighing on her mind. You see, she has always carried a heavy soul. My husband and I often described her as "the wisdom of an older woman pressed into a young girl's heart."

Past experiences of our late-night chats included Kaete sharing a situation where a friend behaved in a way that was scary to her. Another time she called me in when a friend threatened to no longer be her friend if she didn't do what the friend told her. Or the time when she thought a friend was being hurt by someone and she wanted to know how to protect her friend while also keeping safe boundaries for herself.

In those moments, I would comfort her, agree to protect her and her friends, to hold her secret (if appropriate), and to not let any further harm come to her or anyone else. In the dark, we could talk through her fear, manage big emotions, and end our time with her feeling safe enough to handle the situation. All the previous late-night visits had proved she could handle her fear with courage, set clear boundaries, and come to terms with the reality that she might lose a friend or two in the process.

As I walked toward her room, I imagined the drama that could be surrounding her in school. She was three months into her freshman year. Her older brother had graduated from the same high school six months earlier and I felt confident that I understood the worries of a high school student.

Maybe a friend is in trouble. Maybe she and her boyfriend since 7th grade broke up. Breakups are common for kids her age. Maybe her class load is too hard or perhaps too easy. Knowing how much Kaete loved challenges, the latter was unlikely.

Maybe someone is bullying her. Smiling, I remembered how she had responded to bullying in kindergarten, yelling at the attacking student, *"You must be hurting inside!"* or in 8th grade, when the principal asked what she thought would be fair restitution for an act against her and she said, *"I want him to take responsibility for what he did and apologize to me face to face."* Loving, kind, and accountable, that was Kaete.

Slowly I opened the door to her dark room. I was instantly soothed as I breathed in the scent of her shampoo and the fabric softener on her bedding. I climbed onto the white iron bed that had been mine as a child. The bed creaked and moved slightly under my weight as snuggled up next to her. She scooted toward me and allowed me to wrap her up in my arms like I did when she was younger, just under my nose and lips so I could soak her in. She lay in my arms quietly and I could feel the tickle of her hair on my face and neck. Her skin was warm and soft. She was leaning into me for comfort. We lay in silence for quite a few minutes before she quietly began crying.

I stroked her hair and asked, *"What's going on?"*

I waited.

She whispered between tears, *"It's really bad."*

I took a breath. *"Is someone hurting you?"*

"No."

Relief. *"Is someone else being hurt?"*

"No."

Confused. *"Did you hurt someone?"*

"No."

Nothing made sense. I felt her emotion, but my brain couldn't come up with a familiar story so I began with, *"You're safe. Whatever it is, you can handle it."*

Again, I waited. The moments seemed like hours as they passed by.

Crying even harder, she said, *"I think I'm pregnant."*

I attempt to comprehend the words, as my brain played short clips of recent events from the past days, weeks, and the calculations of her 14 years of life. Only hours earlier, I had taken the trash from her bathroom and noticed, for the second week in a row, no evidence of her having her period. I wrote off that observation to a change in activity after completing a sports season and having more down time.

My menstrual cycle was always out of sync when I was her age. I would oftentimes go months without a cycle during the school year. My brain found evidence to create a safe story and I believed it.

In those brief moments, I recalled a few weeks earlier when she had asked to attend her brother's regatta with me and her dad. She stayed close by my side, just like when she was a little girl and felt afraid about something. I thought back, remembering it had been odd that she hadn't asked if her boyfriend, Erick, could go along. But I had been happy to have her all to ourselves for a day. My brain wondered if there was another reason for her regression.

I replayed a conversation she and I had recently had about sex, waiting, and defining loving relationships in teenage years. Knowing these conversations were awkward and uncomfortable for both of us, I had staged a moment in the car to talk about how I had noticed she and her boyfriend were sitting a little bit closer. She and I talked about sex – when it is appropriate to have sex, and with whom. I felt proud of her responses: that they had been talking about it and both wanted to wait. I remembered holding comfort in the *wait* part of the conversation, totally oblivious to the *we have been talking about it*.

From the comfort of her bed, I started thinking about what her father and I did when we were dating and he had become comfortable with me, just as I had witnessed Erick becoming more comfortable with Kaete. I felt a shift as my mind raced, throwing random thoughts in the air that I shot down like I was skeet shooting to control Kaete's life.

She's scared. Aim...FIRE! *Her period is late.*

She doesn't make things up. Aim...FIRE! *She's just tired.*

Something is different here. Aim...FIRE! *Her boyfriend is too shy to try anything.*

In my heart, I could feel it. Something was different. No matter how many excuses my brain could find to shoot down the evidence in front of me, I couldn't escape the fact that I was lying in Kaete's bed holding her as she cried. My baby was scared. I began to cry, too.

She's so young. I kept holding her.

She can't be. I kept holding her.

I am going to lose her. I kept holding her.

She has more to say. I kept holding her.

As I continued to hold her, I reminded her that she was safe. It was okay to say what she needed to say. And *if* she was pregnant, we would get through it together, as a family. It was a big IF. I wouldn't let myself believe it was true. Yet as I held her, I could sense she was confident it was a strong possibility.

I started the conversation again, asking if she had taken a pregnancy test. She hadn't.

I asked her how many weeks late her period was. *"Two weeks."*

I waited and held my breath, wondering if it was possible. The thing about Kaete is that she was born due north. The kind of child who was clear on moral truth and integrity. She never wavered in who she was, even as a toddler. She was observant and empathetic as a preschooler. She was straightforward and loving in elementary school. She was confident and determined in middle school. She remained honest, pure-hearted, and clear on right and wrong.

There has never been a doubt who she is and who she will grow to be. These truths created even more confusion in my head around "typical teenage sexual behavior" and me wanting to rescue her innocence from the world around her.

As my mind drifted through thoughts, Kaete opened her worry-filled heart.

"I'm scared, Mom." She started.

"What are you scared of?" I still refused to believe it.

She began to cry. *"What if Jesus doesn't love me anymore?"*

I cried as I felt the breath being sucked from my body and understood her fear was not about having a baby, it was about being loved. It was the wrenching honesty of courage it took to open up her heart to me and to wonder if she would still be loved.

"Honey, Jesus knew about this baby long before you or I were created. He knows you and loves you. No matter what."

Through sniffles, she said, *"Okay,"* and relaxed slightly.

"What else are you scared of?" I asked.

She started crying harder as she answered, *"What if no one ever wants to work with you again because I got pregnant?"* She was referring to my private practice and training of other parents and educators. She was taking on the responsibility of my business's success. I felt venom build in me as I imagined someone judging our family so harshly that they wouldn't want to work with me again.

Firmly I responded, *"I don't care. I don't want to work with those people."*

She was thinking about me and my work and all I could think about was her and the courage it took for her to say everything she had to say that night.

Her body relaxed and I stayed with her until we were both breathing calmly. As she began to drift off to sleep, I asked her if she needed anything else before I kissed her goodnight. Beginning to softly cry again, she said, *"Will you tell Dad?"*

Her dad! While I was with her in her room, he was across the hall in our bedroom alone. I had heard him get up once or twice, but I hadn't thought about him until she asked me to share her secret. What would I say to him? How would I possibly start that conversation? What would his response be to the news? It didn't matter. *"Of course I will"* is all I said as I left.

I walked back to my bedroom and began firing shots at myself. *What kind of mother lets her child get pregnant?*

I slid into bed next to my unknowing husband. He rolled toward me, asking if everything was okay. Through tears, I told him everything.

He lay still and quiet as he took in what I was telling him. He's always been still and quiet. Brian is the rock of our family, taking in information and quietly creating a plan to serve us all faithfully and without any doubt. Being in the space of the person I love more than anyone else as he experienced the pain of what I shared was loving and quiet. Out loud, he wondered what he should do. I encouraged him to go to her. She needed to know how much he loved her. He was uncomfortable, scared, and sad... but he loves his daughter deeply. So, he went.

two | *Tests*

Whatever season you're in, whatever life may throw at you, whether it feels like success or like failure, expected or unexpected, you have been made ready.
Joanna Gaines

It was past midnight. I sat on the bed my baby used to climb into in the middle of the night in order to be close. The same bed her daddy would pick her up from to carry her back to her own, no matter how big she grew. Now it was where her daddy and I sat, plotting where we could buy a pregnancy test that we were least likely to see anyone we knew from our small community. We looked up the hours of the local pharmacy. We researched the accuracy of every test on the market. We discussed the importance of a test that said PREGNANT rather than showing one or two lines. This was not a time to have to question the results. Before we fell back to sleep, we had a plan: Wake up early and head straight to the drugstore.

I slept soundly, which surprised me later, given the circumstances. Over my years of parenting, I had found myself sleeping less than my body required, spending many nights thinking anxious thoughts, replaying my responses, or generally worrying about my children. As I woke, I wondered if God had given me a break, knowing what He knew. Or maybe it was pure exhaustion and the truth that there was nothing I could do regardless of the outcome of a pregnancy test.

In the mundane moments of coffee-drinking, brushing my teeth, and attempting small talk with Brian, I was overcome with the weight of the fact that life could be different. Though it seemed dramatic, I knew I was experiencing something that was changing my outlook on life, parenting, teen parents, and my family, moment by moment.

I felt an internal shift so deeply that I began to shake. *I want to redo the past 15 years of life, to give Kaete more information about sex... maybe more comfort or freedom to discuss it... Maybe I could have tried harder to connect with Erick when he visited our home... Maybe I could have set clear limits on the amount of time they spent together... Maybe I could have... Maybe... Maybe...*

I was blaming myself for all of it. These thoughts were different than the parenting guilt I had previously experienced. I felt scared as I took on the responsibility for ruining my child's life.

Brian and I climbed into his truck and drove directly to the drugstore in silence. We walked inside just as an employee unlocked the doors. The lights were blindingly bright and up-beat music was playing overhead. Cashiers greeted us with smiles as the urge to hit them and scream welled up inside me so intensely that I looked away and simply read the overhead signs pointing us in the direction of *Life is going to change for you if your daughter pees on this stick.*

We walked down the aisle where pregnancy tests are sold and were overwhelmed by the options. Nothing we had researched was sold in this store.

Google had betrayed us. We stood and read box after box, finally opting for the most expensive, most accurate, easiest to read pregnancy test on the market... in a two-pack.

I walked to the cashier with this weight in my hand, feeling confused. The last time I bought a pregnancy test, I was full of excitement and anticipation, thinking of all the cute ways I could surprise my husband with the news of our growing family. My ideas were full of magic and romance – the moments I now see on social media where everyone gives an *"Awwww"* and Oprah invites you on her show. This moment was filled with a different kind of anticipation. Dread replaced excitement. Dr. Phil replaced Oprah.

The cashier saw the pregnancy test and got a twinkle in her eye as she looked at us. She gave us our total, we paid, and she sent us on our way with a jolly *Have a great day!* or *Good luck!* or something I forget now because all I felt like doing was telling her to *Fuck off!* Instead I politely smiled and walked out with my husband.

On the drive home, I made a smart-ass comment about the cashier thinking we were having a baby and how that would be sooooo much worse. My beloved shot me down with a stare I've seen only a few times since the moment we met in high school. I gazed out the window as I recognized my pattern for sarcasm when situations feel out of control. The remaining six-block drive home was silent.

As soon as we arrived home, we woke Kaete and sent the newly purchased test kit into the bathroom with her. We waited in the hall outside as I again thought of the last time I anticipated the results of a pregnancy test. Two minutes seemed like eternity. This time, we were face to face with the results within moments, as our daughter opened the door and handed me the stick. Positive.

She stood staring at her father and me as if she already knew but was waiting for the information to sink into our bones. We broke down into tears and sandwiched her between us. There she stood, firm and certain.

We pulled back and I asked, *"What do you want to do?"* I hoped and prayed she would say, *"Stay home and be rocked by you, Mommy."* Instead, she responded flatly, *"I want to go to school,"* as if there were no other option for how she would spend her day. She wanted to be with her peers, not her parents. She wanted life to be normal, not weird. At home, it was going to be different and she already knew this. She walked into her room and immediately sent a text to Erick sharing the results.

We stood in the hallway in silence as we waited for her to emerge ready for school. I sent a brief text to Erick: *"We are not angry or upset. Whatever happens, we will get through this together. We love you."* He responded: *"Thank you. Love you, too."* I couldn't help but wonder, *Does he believe us? Does he know we will be here? Can he handle doing this?* Then I wondered, *Do I believe us? Can we be there for him? Can I handle this?* I no longer knew myself. How could I be confident with him while feeling so confused? We knew so little about him other than what we had observed in our home.

By this time in their relationship, he had been hanging out at our house for well over a year, keeping a respectful space between himself and Kaete on our couch. I would catch glimpses of them as he watched her with a gentle smile while she talked and talked, engaging in conversation with her only when we left the room. He respected our rules and, from what we saw, relaxed Kaete and made her laugh.

I fantasized that this pregnancy would provide the opportunity for us to build a deeper relationship with him. I do this through conversation and listening to the heart of the person I'm talking with. Without conversation, my brain creates drama and I believe my creation. I began to visualize a fantasy relationship with Erick where we both talked openly about *everything*. I needed to believe this new relationship could exist to release me from the guilt I was placing on myself, and that this 14-year-old boy could parent a baby.

In those moments in the hallway, with Kaete on the other side of the door, I remembered stories of girls getting pregnant and then being dumped by their boyfriends, leaving the girl and her parents to raise the baby alone. These stories made my head spin as I replayed judgments and mockery. I felt dizzy in my desire to control the stories before they could control us.

My daughter will not be a mockery. I convinced Brian we should tell the school counselor that morning before anyone else could. Twenty minutes later, the three of us drove to the high school in silence.

The walk from the parking lot to the counselor's office felt excruciatingly slow. It was as if I were being physically pulled in the opposite direction of my motion, yet the mental pull to complete the task felt greater. The possibility of being seen and heard was both horrifying and safe. What if the counselor judged me, or my husband or, worst of all, my baby girl? My faith and trust in the world outside my home was shaking and I began laying the first brick in my new wall. It was time to armor up in preparation for the rest of my life as Kaete's mother.

As quickly as I began building that wall, I paused and pivoted my thoughts while I slowly picked the metaphorical brick up and thought, *What if the counselor cries with us? What if we find an ally in this? What if we could be rescued from walking this path?* Years of listening to the fantasies my brain created, followed by telling myself *Just wait*, always revealed possibilities I couldn't fathom. We walked down the hall to learn what our beginning would be.

We greeted the counselor with all the typical pleasantries and sat down, Brian and I on the small sofa, our daughter in a chair. I looked around the room at the certificates, licenses, and family pictures. *Three boys. She'll never have to deal with this.*

As soon as everyone was comfortable, I blurted out the news. Tears began to pour down my face for the third time in less than an hour. Kaete sat expressionless, no response, no eye contact. I imagined her thinking, *So this is how it's going to be? My mom cries uncontrollably at the mention of my name or "the situation"?*

The counselor turned to us and all my worry about whether she would be on our side or not quickly vanished when she looked at Kaete and responded, *"It's just a baby. No one is sick or dying."*

A flat *This is no big deal in the grand scheme of life* while I sat there feeling simultaneously numb and shocked. I imagined her counselor education was a big book of teenage problems where she simply flipped through the pages until she got to the chapter titled "Teen Pregnancy" and recited what she was taught.

Continuing on, she assured Kaete that she was there to help, to share the news when or if it was appropriate, and finished by asking if there was anything else we needed. Nope. Nothing. The first brick was laid.

We told Kaete goodbye as she walked to class, and I rode home with Brian, holding the next brick.

three | *Bricks*

The primary cause of unhappiness is never the situation, but your thoughts about it.
Eckhart Tolle

All I could think about as we drove home in silence were all the ways I have protected Kaete over the years. She's strong, yet I continued to want to save her from any negative feelings, anyone with negative thoughts about her, or anyone who physically tried to harm her. I felt overwhelmed with my inability to provide such protection. The sense of control that feels safe in the moment but holds no hope for the future washed over me. The conflict rising would become significant in how I would move forward. I did want to protect her, but I wanted her to be full of courage and brave enough to face whatever was coming even more.

In those few blocks, I became aware of my husband's pain and the weight of a situation we never in a million years would have seen coming. I glanced in his direction and could see he was on the brink of crying. I turned away for fear I would lose control of all emotional balance I was feeling.

We were together in the car yet totally apart. Every dream or story I had created about Kaete's high school years was slowly drifting away, being replaced by stories I had said myself about teen parents. It was going to be *a hard life*. Having watched just enough reality TV to confirm this, I would not allow it to be Kaete's experience. I grasped for any thoughts that could change the story of my pain. *Kaete was created for this moment. Kaete is a hard worker. Kaete will know exactly what to do. Kaete has a life full of support and love.*

We arrived home and entered our kitchen from the garage as I realized, *I have a life full of support and love.* I sent a text to my friend: *"Kaete's pregnant."*

I didn't expect a response, nor did I know how to carry on a conversation in my current state of emotions and questions surrounding my daughter's future. Yet within 20 minutes, my friend was standing in our kitchen hugging me and Brian, holding our fears, and loving each of us as we wrapped our brains around the truth.

My friend had been there with her son his junior year of high school when he learned his girlfriend was pregnant. She had sat with the counselor, walked her child through teen pregnancy, and embraced her grandchild with love. She knew what we were going through, and shared words that Brian and I would hold on to as an anchor whenever our emotions started to toss us around: *"It will be hard, and then it will be easier, and then it will be hard again. But when the baby arrives, everything is better."* Eventually these words would become the truth that would reveal itself.

My friend returned to work, leaving us sobbing and holding each other in our kitchen. Questioning who we were, what we had missed, what we could do, and how to move forward. One by one, I was silently laying bricks and didn't want to stop. With each brick, I believed I could create safety to protect our family from judgment. Yet these so-called safety bricks weren't stopping me from judging myself. Blindly I laid bricks, keeping those judgments on the same side of my new wall. No way to escape.

four | *Distances*

*Empathy is not about happiness. It is about owning our
feelings instead of projecting them onto others.*
Dr. Becky A. Bailey

Kaete was attending school on a Thursday as
if it was any other day. Fourteen years old, three
months into her freshman year, and pregnant. I, on
the other hand, realized I was scheduled to leave on a
work trip.

I considered cancelling, for fear Kaete would
need me and I would be too far away to help. After
many hours discussing my options, Brian assured me
he could handle anything and that it might even be
good for me to go. He knew me well enough to know

I needed to sleep and create space to think, and he knew my friends would wrap me in love and support me when I couldn't support myself.

I sent an email to the friends I would be seeing soon and asked them to help me through the training, to take good notes, and to keep my secret safe unless I was the one talking about it. Kaete and Erick assured me they would tell his parents about the pregnancy while I was gone.

A two-hour layover in Atlanta provided the right amount of distance I needed to protect myself, and the strangers passing by gave a sense of anonymity I hadn't felt up to that point. In my anxiety-induced state, I chose a large carpeted area in the Atlanta airport as the best place to call my parents. This quiet corner was away from foot traffic and loud overhead announcements, and had comfortable seating. No one would be joining me. Sitting on the newly installed bright carpet, I propped myself against the wall and, one by one, called my family to tell them about the pregnancy before they heard it from someone else.

Each phone call was the same. I cried through the news. The person on the other end referred to Kaete and Erick with statements of pity (*"problem"*; *"so young"*; *"What a shame"*; *"Will they stay together?"*; *"What is she going to do?"*). I gave short responses as I closed my heart a little bit and felt the wall of protection growing brick by brick, unknowingly keeping Kaete on the other side while believing I was holding her close.

Arriving in Florida, I immediately reached for my phone to connect with the friends I had notified before I left home. Each of them held my emotions, listened to my heart, kept me talking, encouraged me to participate when I felt like crawling away, and helped me understand training material I could not retain. A few found a way to bring me closer to truths I was denying about my worth, Kaete and Erick's choices, and the stories I was creating out of fear. They supported me and walked with me every step of the way.

I ended each day talking late into the night with the roommate I had chosen eight months prior. We knew each other through years of working together, and I remembered she had a similar story. We were both surprised at the unknown importance of our roommate choice all those months ago. Her experience, and ability to hold my overwhelming emotions, began to chip away at my brick wall.

The business of being in the presence of others was a chore. It had its benefits (distraction) and its struggles (vulnerability), yet I could sense I was exactly where I needed to be. I would look around the room and see love, not pity. When I would feel a wave of sadness wash over me, I could feel a shift in the friend sitting near me. Her body language offered comfort and the freedom to be with others who knew nothing but had heard *something*. Together we laughed, danced, ate, drank, learned, grew, and created.

Near the end of the training, as the group discussed setting boundaries, I asked the leader how to protect children when you are actively watching them hurt. Her words became a lifeline I returned to when my emotions were overwhelming or I unfairly turned on myself.

"We cannot protect them, but we can be there for them when they need us." She went on, *"You must find people in your life to help you manage your emotions so you can be present for her without burdening her. She has enough to deal with."*

I arrived home feeling more resilient, and shared the wise words with Brian. He agreed that we had a strong support system and we would be able to get through this together. I asked him if Kaete and Erick had told Erick's parents. They hadn't. I felt anger and resentment wash over me, wanting to know why they were all still stuck – then paused, remembering the words I had shared only moments before: *She has enough to deal with.*

five | *Calls*

You don't have to control your thoughts, you just have to stop letting them control you. Dan Millman

Each day I woke with a curious awareness and wondering. *Who will I talk to? What will their expression be as they talk to me?* I sensed other people's responses through their facial cues and body language as I prepared for what was about to be expressed. Sometimes I was surprised by the matter-of-fact tone that felt loving. *"Oh man, that could be any of us." "You guys can do this."* And sometimes it was filled with judgment. *"Well, I guess that happens…"* allowed me to fill dead air space: *"with careless parents"; "but I'm so glad it's you and not me"; "just not to me."* This same ability to sense emotions was going to be lost on the one person I had yet to tell. My son.

Jace had left for college just a few months earlier. We had frequently spent time with him at collegiate football games or when his rowing crew raced in area regattas. He and I are very similar in our patterns of thinking and being in this world. We love similarly, we find similar humor in the mundane, and we sense others in a unique way that is unfortunately often accurate. I missed seeing and talking with him every day. As much as I didn't want to call him, I missed his voice, and I realized I had to, before one of his high school friends heard the news and told him. *Turns out high school boys have more discretion regarding privacy than grown women.*

Not being allowed to see and sense his response when I called left me full of grief and guilt, as memories of him and Kaete flashed through my mind. Jace, with a huge smile, holding baby Kaete. Jace and Kaete riding their bikes, holding puppies, playing in the yard, and on vacations. Kaete cheering Jace through years of swimming. Jace teasing Kaete relentlessly as she whined his name in two syllables,

Ja-ace! They were a sibling set I had never experienced before and I could feel the magnitude of the news.

I stood in the middle of my kitchen, gaining the courage and finding the words to tell him Kaete was pregnant. When I could no longer deny the importance of his knowing, I looked at his contact picture on my phone and, with shaking hands, I called.

"Do you have a minute to talk?"

Upbeat and smiling through the phone as usual, he responded, *"Sure! What's up?"*

Flatly, I asked *"Where are you? What are you doing?"*

"I'm in the Union... What's going on?" His voice was laced with concern and curiosity as he waited for me to find my breath and words through the tears that were beginning to work their way to the surface. I assured him, *"Everyone is safe."*

"So what's going on?" He was growing more concerned by my tears.

"Kaete's pregnant."

"What? Just a minute." He was looking for a place to sit. A place to stop his world from shrinking

in around him. And then he said again, *"What?"*

I repeated myself and cried and felt his anger and sadness all bound up in his distance from home. Completely unable to do anything else, we spoke a few brief sentences and then he *had to go*.

I set my phone on the countertop and slid to the floor. Sobbing, with my face in my hands, I was overcome with shame. I couldn't save Kaete and I couldn't save my son. What good was I as a parent? The shame and relentless feelings of anger kept washing over me, directed at no one but myself.

We couldn't know this wouldn't be the last time I would be the one to give him news that would shake and upend his world. Nearly two years later, I would call him at work to tell him that his roommate had taken his own life. These two moments created a pattern – I am no longer allowed to call him without a text first.

I had spent 19 years as a mother with one promise in mind: *Keep them safe*. I had kept them safe from abuse, from drugs, from being perpetrated against. I had kept them safe from boredom and laziness. I had kept them safe from injury and dismemberment. But I couldn't keep them safe from their emotions.

Sitting alone in my kitchen, I was completely surrounded by thoughts that it was over. *Everything we knew as a family was over* began to play on repeat until I calmed and paused. I had experienced deep emotion before and could reflect on what thoughts were helpful. As I sat slowly breathing, I remembered previously finding calm in the thought, *"One year from now…,"* and there it was again. *"One year from now… I will be holding a baby on the floor of my kitchen."* And just like that, the moment changed. The school counselor was right. *It's only a baby.*

six | *Plans*

You know, sometimes all you need is twenty seconds of insane courage. Benjamin Mee

"*Have you told them yet?*"

I watched Erick from my rearview mirror as I drove him home from school the day before Kaete's first doctor appointment.

He shook his head.

For nearly three weeks, Brian and I had waited for Erick to tell his parents. We had him over for dinner and reminded him to tell them. We included him in routine chores and mundane daily activity with our family, hoping he believed us when we told him we loved him and would get through this together. We drove him to and from his house exactly how we had in the weeks prior, each time believing it would be the night he would tell his parents.

This time I explained that Brian and I needed someone to confide in and partners on the journey. In a last-ditch effort, I reminded him that he needed parental permission to be excused from school to attend the appointment. He had told Kaete he wanted to attend every doctor appointment. Driving him toward his home, the realization hit me: He was a boy who couldn't drive. A boy who needed his parents' consent to leave school. A boy who was going to be a father.

Later that same night, Erick would walk into his parents' bedroom repeatedly, turning to leave when they inquired what he wanted at that hour. After multiple attempts, he stood in the doorway and told them Kaete was pregnant. It was his mom's birthday.

The next morning, Erick's parents dropped him off at our house while Brian and I waited for Kaete to get ready for school. Always very quiet, but typically comfortable, he walked into our house with his face tight, looking down as he held his hands together. Confused, I asked him if he was okay as he leaned over a chair in our dining room. He smiled tightly and nodded. Brian and I looked at each other and shrugged. We expected him to feel uncomfortable and unsure, but we hadn't expected what we now saw.

The three of us stood quietly, waiting for Kaete to come down from her bedroom. When she popped into the room, he turned to her, holding out his thumb that was swollen and red. He explained that he had shut it in the door of his mother's car. Though I was relieved to know he wasn't in excruciating *emotional* pain, I had no idea if his injury required medical attention – but given the timing of his injury, I didn't really care. We had somewhere to go and my brain needed us to move forward.

We drove in silence to the office, where a stranger would perform a sonogram on my baby girl and give us a due date for how far along the pregnancy was. All four of us sat in the waiting room of a clinic full of older Mennonite patients and staff. "Classic country" music played overhead. I reminded everyone how much I hate country music. Erick sat painfully, still squeezing his thumb with his other hand. Always the talker, I teased him about the thumb, then poked at it with genuine concern at the rapid swelling and discoloration. And then it was time to go back to the examining room.

The sonographer had difficulty hearing or seeing the tiny heartbeat from her exterior search. For the first time, I found myself fearful that something might have happened to the little life. Up until this moment, I had bounced between praying that it wasn't real and hoping that whatever happened, Kaete would feel loved and supported.

The technician decided to perform an internal sonogram. She described what this was to the four of us and we left the room for Kaete to get into a hospital gown. Soon after we reentered the room, right on the black-and-white screen was the tiniest little flicker of a heartbeat. The life created in young love was flashing in front of us. As all of us stared and smiled in amazement, so much of our fear disappeared.

Once Erick finally told his parents that Kaete was pregnant, Brian and I felt known and understood in only the way two other parents in the exact same situation in life could. We immediately invited them to dinner.

Two days later, we sat across from Erick's parents, Sol and Vivis, at a local restaurant, surrounded by our community. We ordered our meals and Vivis told us the story of Erick coming into their room the night of her birthday as Sol interpreted her words. She laughed as she shared the story – *"In and out, in and out"* – using gestures for emphasis as she described Erick building the courage to tell them. All the while, her face held apology. Vivis is tiny and truthful, and looked at Sol for confirmation in respect and validation. Sol replied and interpreted with love and tears, as Vivis watched and listened to every word we said, nodding in solidarity.

Before that day, we had only met at school functions or during drop-offs and pick-ups as our children dated. Our relationship was polite and kind, a simple *"Hello"* and *"How are you?"* in our own languages. Previously, I had never considered the importance of our ability to communicate. I believed that middle-school relationships typically expire, and that kept us from getting to know each other better.

During the meal, we learned more about who they are as individuals, parents, and a couple. We shared our personal stories of dating. They began dating when they were 15 years old, Brian and I when he was 15 and I was 17. Together we laughed and cried through the similarities, understanding why Kaete and Erick wanted to spend so much time together.

We believed in our children, yet knew how much support they would need to be successful. So, the four of us began devising a plan for our children's lives without their input. Sol and Vivis wanted Erick to get a job and to get good grades. Brian and I wanted both kids to do everything they planned to do in school, considering there would be time for jobs later in life. Sol and Vivis apologized repeatedly, as we assured them over and over that we held no blame. We knew the two kids liked each other A LOT and no amount of teaching, instructing, discussing, or sharing consequences seemed to make a difference. We were in it together and we could be a team.

We finished our meal and agreed to share with

our children *The Plan* we had devised. Brian and I paid for the meal in celebration and appreciation... which was the start of a long-running battle between Brian and Sol to "get the tab." (I still don't know how they manage to remember from one meal to the next who paid for what, yet this humorous tradition continues.)

A few days later, Brian, Kaete, and I joined Erick, his parents, and two of his three brothers in the living room of their home. One brother was away on a mission for their church. The oldest brother was there to interpret if needed, and the younger brother present as witness. Erick's parents and brothers sat on dining chairs they had brought into the room. Comfortable and smiling, Kaete snuggled up to Erick on the couch as Erick leaned toward her with ease. Brian and I sat on the loveseat. I wanted to crawl onto his lap and press my head against his chest to feel the vibration of his deep voice and soothing heartbeat. Instead I sat next to him like a grown woman and held his right hand tightly between my two.

We and Erick's parents shared *The Plan* we created for Kaete and Erick's life: They would continue to attend school and be involved in any sports or extracurricular activities they wanted, and we would support them and help them be successful. Sol shared his desire for Erick to work hard and get good grades, while I expressed my wish for the kids to love and respect each other *no matter what happened* (insinuating they might break up). These big expectations were a lot to hold for two young teens, yet they sat there soaking it all in, looking at us with innocent smiles and sweet glances toward each other.

Sol took a deep breath as he readied himself to speak again. After a few long seconds, he looked up through teary eyes and softly said, *"It is good to see Kaete smile."* He proceeded to share that in the few weeks prior, he would see her in his rearview mirror as she rode along, quiet and sad. He compared this to her behavior in the past and the joy that was evident as she sang with the radio or talked and laughed with Erick in the back of their van.

Sol knew something was different, but he didn't know what until he learned about her pregnancy. He offered another teary smile when he looked at us and acknowledged how good it was to see her happy again.

My body relaxed and my cheeks felt warm as I began to love this gentle man who would be the grandfather of a baby we had yet to meet. *He knows love and he knows my girl.* Sitting in their warm living room sharing our babies with each other felt safe. It was exactly how family should be.

seven | *Supports*

How people treat you is on them. How you react is on you.
Aniesa Hanson

On the morning we found out Kaete was pregnant, my friend stood in my kitchen and told me, *"During this time, you will find out who your true friends are... and just how hurtful your family can be."* I thought it trite at the time, but it would turn out she was right.

Acquaintances and old friends were empathetic, kind, and thoughtful. They knew what they could handle and appeared to know what I could handle when it came to listening, questioning, or sharing. So I was surprised when a family member entered our home as we were setting the table for dinner and announced, *"[Child's name] said she has lost all respect for Kaete."* I stopped and stared silently. The talking continued. *"I told her, 'That's fine. You don't have to respect her.'"*

Kaete was in the same room. I glanced in her direction. *Are you hearing this!?* I silently prayed: *Please, God, make her deaf to this.* I stood frozen, waiting for this fling of hatred to leave my home. I couldn't comprehend the purpose of this visit. Was she trying to teach me a lesson? *If you don't fit the mold of what we believe in, we lose all belief in you.* Or maybe, *My kids are better than yours and I'll stand by that.* It didn't make any sense. There was little more said before this person exited our home. It was painful, and it was over.

As I walked back into the kitchen to finish getting dinner on the table, perfect snarky responses started coming to me. I could have said, *"Before you open your mouth, please think, Is what I am about to share going to help this family feel supported, loved, and encouraged? Or is it going to help me feel better for a few minutes?"* My heart couldn't take any more. I found myself spiraling deeper into doubt and shame in my ability to parent.

I was the subject of gossip being spread about my child by family and community members, and people who knew Erick's family. There were so many hurtful words, sprinkled with a few bits of tepid kindness. *What a shame. It's not right. No respect. It should have been me. It could happen to anyone. That better not happen to my son/daughter! I don't know how you do it. I could never do it.* Comments swirled around me on repeat. Kaete's pregnancy was no one else's story, yet I held those stories with love toward those who judged, and increased anxiety in me each time I listened.

Those comments continued to swirl as mothers shared painful stories of abuse, abandonment, or judgment by family members, along with their own experiences as teen parents and how the dad didn't stick around. I heard from women who got married at 15, 16, or 17 years old, only to be abused, live with an addict, or never reach their dreams. Everywhere I went, I received and held their stories of hurt with love. But with their release, my fears about Kaete and Erick's relationship grew, as bricks stacked higher in an invisible fortress of protection.

More pain arrived when I sat in the living room of a friend who asked if Kaete was pregnant. I thought, *I was coming to confide in you, and my confidence was broken by gossip,* as she explained how she heard the news from a cheer-mom whose daughter was on the same squad as Kaete.

As my friend told me the grapevine of news, I felt myself split. On one side of me was care and concern; on the other, sharp pain from others owning my family's story. *We are making the news and people feel compelled to talk about it.* A rush of anger washed over me, aimed at everyone who was sharing my family's information without coming through me first. I had guilty flashes to all the times I had told news that wasn't mine to share, yet empathized with the thrill of gossip. I silently vowed from then on never to do this.

With this personal boundary set in place, I knew I would need to find the words to sit firmly with it as others shared Kaete and Erick's private information. Holding to this, I went home and sent a text to all the friends in the news-loop, asking them to contact me before they spread information about our family. A boundary drawn with those I trusted made me feel safe and able to move forward.

Friends rallied around me. Some were supportive at basketball games, where I felt free to answer questions, and others reached out by email or phone. Others stopped me in the grocery store or the high school parking lot, hugging me as we both cried.

We reminisced how, "just moments before," we had driven our girls to choir practice and then gone to drink margaritas, so that our husbands had to come pick us up when practice ended. "Just moments before," we had been working out with our girls in preparation for high school volleyball. "Just moments before," we'd gone shopping for middle-school formal dresses. "Just moments before," we had been having coffee and discussing what "age-appropriate relationships" should be. "Just moments before," we had been making plans for how we'd use our freedom as our youngest children entered high school.

Now I faced each friend not knowing what my future held, certainly unsure that freedom would be available once a baby entered my world. Sometimes I sat with these friends sharing parts of the story that weren't mine. Telling my feelings as they came to me. Craving a sense of "normal development," where I could continue to raise my daughter and be free from judgment.

The desire for normalcy pushed us to attend the collegiate basketball games of our good friends' daughter, just as we had in years prior. When Kaete was in 7th grade, our families had vacationed together and played Cards Against Humanity, all the while trying to shield Kaete from inappropriate language, topics, and our insanely vulgar comments, to which she'd hilariously responded, *"Guys, I've heard it. I go to public school."*

These friends shared Kaete's news with their children, who reacted with love and protection. Their son would give Erick the evil eye when he saw him in the high school gym, and their daughter would reach out to Kaete, becoming a closer mentor and friend. They all continued to wrap her in love through relentless teasing just as they had her entire life. Watching them embrace her as they always had was comforting. Our lives would be normal, whatever that meant.

More normalcy arrived as I ran with a friend who expressed true love as I blurted out, *"Kaete's pregnant."* She stopped mid-run, looked at me, burst into tears, and said, *"No. She's too young."* She knew how I felt.

This was the first moment I pulled myself away from the situation and felt the weight of my jumbled emotions freely without the need to protect Brian, Jace, Kaete, or Erick. It was the first moment I realized I was not alone in this.

Someone else was bearing the shock and pain with me. Someone who had experienced a similar situation when she was 19 and found herself unexpectedly pregnant. A friend who worked in an obstetrics office and saw so many young mothers come in and out of the office and could share her fears with loving support. A friend who would take a carload of teenage boys to the trampoline park the night Erick smashed his finger and tell me, *"He needs a doctor."* A friend who would bring her words and emotion and make me feel a little less alone. A friend who could hold and bear the weight of my painful anger, grief, and sadness. Not once joining me, but instead freeing me.

The normal moments wove together with painful stories from those who needed to be heard, along with the hopeful stories of marriage and *happily ever after.* Through it all, I held my breath that this story would have a happy ending. It had to.

eight | *Strangers*

This moment, like all moments, is an instant of pure possibility. Tamara Levitt

Emotions continued to swirl through my head as time passed. I became numb to the news traveling. I found myself spending more time alone in an effort to avoid faces, voices, and judgment. I asked fewer questions of Kaete after noticing her irritation with my emotions. I reminded myself that it was not her job to take care of me, and so I stepped back until I could no longer step back. Discomfort found a new meaning in my body as I clenched my jaw and held my breath any time I saw a familiar face.

The date for the first obstetric appointment

arrived. Kaete looked forward to the consistency that would arrive along with it – the consistency of a relationship with a doctor who would listen and watch for every possible concern, and create trust to prepare for an incredibly uncomfortable moment in life. Kaete already knew she wanted her GP to deliver her baby. Dr. Annie had been Kaete's physician for five years and Kaete felt comfort in her care.

Kaete and Erick invited Vivis to hear the baby's heartbeat and to meet the doctor who would deliver our grandchild. In the days between finding out about the pregnancy and this appointment, I had struggled to share Kaete with anyone. I was not ready to share myself, either.

Protection, more bricks, and the fear of absolutely losing my shit kept people at arm's length. Inside, I knew those kinds of relationships weren't going to help Kaete or Erick feel supported. Up until that appointment, I had only spent two brief periods with Erick's parents – first at the restaurant and then in their home. I pivoted my thoughts and found a way to view the invitation as a rite of passage... a chance to spend more time with Vivis, and for us to learn how to support our children.

The morning of the appointment, I let my emotions and fears slip away in recognition of what was important to Kaete and her relationship with her unborn baby's family. She has always liked a plan, so I prepared her for the appointment by giving her and Erick specific instructions about what time and where I would pick them up from school. With my newfound strength and a plan in place, I agreed to give Vivis a ride. *I can handle this!* I silently exclaimed.

The afternoon of the appointment, I paced the house and stared at the clock as the scheduled time for Vivis to arrive came and went. Kaete called to see when I was coming. I assured her we would *"be there any minute."* The second I hung up the phone, I saw Erick's aunt's car turn the corner. With a leap, I went to the garage and pulled my car out. Assuming Vivis had caught a ride with her sister, I jumped out of my car and waved her over. However, she didn't get out when they pulled up.

As I slowly walked toward the street, I realized the car was full of women from Erick's family, who apparently would be joining us. I encouraged them to follow me in my car or meet me at the clinic, but they insisted I drive their car and we all pick Kaete and Erick up together. I wanted to walk away with a *"No, thank you!"* There were too many people for my comfort, yet I had no idea how to say, *"I can't do this. It's overwhelming. I need space!"*

So, I agreed. I climbed into the driver's seat next to Vivis, joining her sister, a niece, the niece's baby, and her oldest son's girlfriend. This was different from my own pregnancies, when just Brian and I attended all our appointments, then talked about what had occurred and if it was newsworthy for our families. If so, we shared. If not, we went on. But this was not my pregnancy. This was not Brian and me. This was Kaete and, as a minor, she needed me to drive and to pay her doctor bills. And Erick needed his family for support.

As I drove the carload toward the high school, Erick's cousin leaned forward and looked at me in the mirror.

"Are you excited about being a grandma?!?" she happily asked.

I felt my stomach tighten as I looked back at

her flatly and said, *"No. Not yet."*

I saw her mother glance at her with a look that encouraged her to be quiet. The cousin sat back. I never appreciated any glance more in my life.

We arrived at the high school and I sent a text to Kaete letting her know we were outside. They loaded up and I drove the full car to the appointment. I was quiet and polite, but it was all I could bear.

My insides tightened as I held onto my wall of bricks through fake responses and surface smiles. I worked hard to manage my emotions as I bounced between wanting to cry and wanting to scream. What was going on? Why was I so confused in a car full of strangers who were already anticipating the life that was created while I was dripping with fear? What was wrong with *me*? What was wrong with *them*?

In the waiting room, we were all sitting in silence when, without warning, Vivis asked Erick when Brian and I had found out about the pregnancy. He shrugged off her question without answering and stared at the floor. I looked to Erick's aunt, who interpreted the question. Quickly I blurted, *"Three weeks."* She shot him a glance that reminded me instantly it wasn't my place to respond.

Vivis began speaking rapidly to Erick in Spanish, and I chuckled at their exchange. As I watched Erick talk with his mother, I realized how little I knew about him, his family, or his capacity to love. Though I couldn't understand the words, I could feel the emotional connection. I was witnessing the persistence of a shy 14-year-old boy and the integrity in his heart. He was going to make a great father.

Kaete and Erick were called back into the exam room. Not long after, the nurse returned to invite the rest us. We all crammed into the tiny room just as Dr. Annie found the thumping of a strong little life. Another shift was occurring inside me. As my body relaxed, tears formed. I looked at Vivis and a smile came across my face. In that moment, the strangers in that room became family. A weird little awkward family, joining to help two kids figure out how to parent another human together.

nine | *Fears*

The question is not what you look at, but what you see.
Henry David Thoreau

"I'm happy for her."

I couldn't believe what he was saying!

Kaete continued to cheer and Erick continued to play basketball. As the season moved along, her waistline began to expand, and protecting her became my obsession. Looking for the worst in others was my pastime. There was no better way to keep myself from growing and empathizing than to judge others.

As hard as I tried to hate, I began to notice that not everyone was judging her. Sure, there were a few stray looks, points, or giggles. But for the most part,

the bleachers at basketball games were full of people who were looking after their own lives, dealing with their own problems, children, illnesses, and relationships. Kaete was *my* life and how I was going to grow or not during this time was *my* problem.

Kaete and Erick spent every day together at school and every evening together, alternating between our home and his. So, often she was with him at his home – a home where I didn't know the family or what boundaries and values they held dear. A home she loved and spent hours at, only to return home, look at us with sleepy eyes and say, *"Good night,"* or maybe respond, *"Fine,"* after I asked about her day or how she felt. I'd see her eyes light up when she saw him and I watched them dim as she saw us again. I wanted to rescue her from the unknown, an unknown that was mine more than hers.

Inside I tortured myself with stories about how Erick's family treated her or judged her. Some stories included a convincing argument about religious beliefs, which would lead me down a dark hole into certainty that they would wipe out all her

previous truth and replace it with new convincing proof that theirs was the best and only way to God. The worst of my imagination was when I convinced myself that their discussions in her presence would make her feel shame or humiliation.

I would keep my worry-induced, crazy ideas mostly to myself, until I had to release them out of sheer panic to be understood. I would share my twisted stories only with close friends who would validate my worries based solely on the information I presented. *"Young women from their church want to talk with her"* or *"I don't know enough about what they believe"* could get my friends on my side quickly. They would join my "I must win Kaete" competition without me having to ask. It was so gratifying when my troops would rally around me and join the battle. But when I returned home, the excitement of the battle disappeared and the stories started up again.

I reached out to Brian, knowing there was only one more person experiencing exactly what I was. I believed he would join the battle just as my girlfriends had, that he would find familiarity in the stories, hold me close, and together we would declare

war. He listened quietly, nodding occasionally, and offering small words of condolence – *"Mm, hmm"* and *"Yeah"* in his soft-spoken loving way.

But his face did not waver. He didn't show the battle-ready twinkle in the eye or the furrow of the brows I desperately waited for. He stared at me with love, laced with a little bit of pity, and responded, *"I'm happy for her."*

I was in shock. I froze, feeling every ounce of my insides unraveling while I questioned my love and commitment to the man standing in front of me. *WHAT?!?! What is he thinking? He's happy for our daughter to be pregnant at 14? He's happy she spends time away from her family who loves her more than anyone else in the world could possibly love her? He's happy that she is giving love to and receiving love from someone else's mother while her own is at home losing her mind?* None of it made any sense.

He's supposed to be on my side! He's supposed to want to protect his daughter! He's supposed to declare war!

Obviously, I hadn't made myself clear. I tried again, spinning the stories, adding more drama to

make him understand why everything about this was bad. He wouldn't have it. He was still happy for her.

I had to get angry and say things that would also make him angry. Point fingers. Create possible worst-case scenarios. He didn't budge.

In the days following, I would tell my friends about Brian's happiness and they would once again join me in my internal war against acts of love and kindness toward Kaete. How could anyone else possibly love my child the way I did? Sure, I loved Erick and could sit and stare at him and Kaete together for hours. I wanted him in my house every night to get to know him better. I wanted to talk with him about his basketball games and to show him love. I wanted him to believe me when I told him that I held no blame or anger or judgment toward him. I saw him as a part of our family, who I didn't ever want to let go. Yet believing his family was loving Kaete in the same way didn't seem feasible.

And then one night, I sat and watched my beautiful, loving girl in the living room of the home of the young man at whom she couldn't stop smiling, after they revealed their baby was a boy. She was talking with his family and sharing stories and inside jokes that had been lived out in Erick's family's home while I was in my own, sinking deeper into loss. Kaete lit up as his parents served her food or brought her something to drink. She laughed with them as they talked openly and freely about the little life inside her.

I fake-smiled through conversations I could only half understand. My stomach tightened while my jaw held firm. I felt as if I was being forced to stay in a situation and could not be released. I knew my desire to get up from the table and storm out of the house was not going to help me, Kaete, or my marriage.

So, I sat and listened. I listened to my husband ask loving questions of Erick's family members. I listened to the responses. Always surprised and craving more, I listened. I listened as if my heart felt what Kaete felt in Erick's home. I listened as they teased Erick and he smiled with embarrassment. I listened as laughter came out of my mouth. And I noticed Kaete's body relax and shift towards me in a silent *Thank you, Mom*. And in that moment, *I* was happy for her.

ten | *Decisions*

*For things to reveal themselves to us, we need to be ready to
abandon our views about them.* Thich Nhat Hanh

Kaete invited Vivis to attend the hospital tour, just as she did with her first doctor appointment. This time around, I knew to ask who all would be coming along. Kaete smiled as she said, *"Probably everyone."* She was right. Vivis and her sister, niece and baby were all in attendance as they followed Kaete, Erick, and me to the hospital in a small town 15 miles away.

Erick's cousin asked the name of the hospital as we arrived and was quick to tell Kaete about her friend who delivered a baby at the same hospital and had *"a terrible experience."* Kaete's face dropped as she thanked the cousin for sharing that.

Our troop walked to the registration desk and asked for the nurse who was meeting us. It had been explained that this nurse would be teaching Kaete and Erick's birthing classes and would ultimately accompany them throughout labor and delivery.

We waited as the woman at the desk looked at me, and then Kaete, before asking, *"Which one of you is expecting?"* I laughed and pointed to my very young-looking daughter, who was wearing a hoodie that covered her baby bump. The woman tightened her lips, looked at Kaete, and said, *"She's on her way,"* before turning back to her work. We waited in the reception area as nurses, technicians, and other hospital staff walked by slowly, looking at our group Not only did the majority of us not *look* like them, I imagined they believed this would never *happen* to them.

The young nurse came around the corner and greeted us with a cheery smile. She wore scrubs and a T-shirt, and her hair in a ponytail. She walked us down the hallway to the birthing suite (actually a single room) as she chatted with Kaete and Erick. The nurse explained the process of checking in during labor, how she would be notified, and how she would notify the doctor. She answered questions about what would happen if there was an emergency. She scheduled the birthing classes with Kaete and Erick. They would be the only two students in attendance.

While we stood in the empty birthing suite, hospital staff walked in and out, performing small tasks. There was no apparent reason for any of them to be in the room with us, but there they were. There was no reason for them to be hanging around the reception desk, but there they were. I kept my eyes on the hospital staff as they roamed around us as Kaete and Erick listened to their nurse explain that this was the only hospital where Dr. Annie delivered.

With this bit of information, Kaete had a decision to make. Where would she deliver her baby? She could deliver in our hometown, where she knew many of the nurses and hospital staff, but that would require she find a new physician. Or she could deliver at the small hospital where she had her first sonogram and would have the physician she loved, Dr. Annie.

Even with the scary stories shared by Erick's cousin, and the awkward stares from hospital staff, Kaete knew if she chose that hospital, she would be choosing her nurse and Dr. Annie. She chose that hospital.

eleven | *Floodgates*

The reason life works at all is because not everyone in your tribe is nuts on the same day.
Anne Lamott

Doctor appointments, school functions, and athletic events were regulars on my schedule and often held during Brian's work hours. When our children were young, we agreed we didn't want to miss anything they were involved in. Whenever possible, Brian would come. However, I had a more flexible job that allowed me to attend almost every event throughout the years. So, all of those years I went. Now, I went for Kaete and I went to prove something to myself and others. I would not be shaken simply because my family's story had changed.

The loneliness of attending without my partner by my side each time was emotionally draining. Month after month and then week after week, I paid for and attended all Kaete's medical visits. I'd sit quietly in the doctor's office listening to Kaete and Erick answer questions, full of anticipation with each measurement of her belly.

Every visit, I heard the doctor and the medical staff encourage and love on Kaete. I was blown away. I expected the office staff to reflect much of society and its judgment passed on teen parents. What I witnessed instead was kindness toward and excitement for our family. Their family.

Many times after these appointments, I felt unable to function mentally after listening to the doctor discuss what was developing in my child's body and what the two kids could expect before the next scheduled appointment. I couldn't separate Kaete's innocence and lack of experience from her old soul and incredible maturity for her age. As her mom, I mourned the loss of her young body and worried about body image issues. I mourned the loss of high school experiences and worried about her getting stuck in a stage of development. I mourned the loss of her freedom and worried about Erick's ability to commit to her and their baby.

Evenings after the appointments, I would cry to Brian and he would apologize for not being able to make the appointments. I would text my fears to my closest friends and they would supportively respond with, *"I don't know how you do it,"* to which I often replied, *"I don't, either."*

And I began wondering...

What else would I do?

What would you do?

Hmmm.

I wanted to see myself and my family in the way others were beginning to express. I watched and lived on the line between perception and comparison. I fought to separate my view of someone else's situation as better than or worse than our current situation. Society told me through media, theory, and education that what we see is what we get. But I was beginning to doubt these truths. I shifted and began to believe we see what we want to see. Society had no idea what was going on within me, or what kind of turmoil occurred to get me to the point of being able to stand upright during an appointment, or to come face to face with someone at a basketball game.

So, I kept attending the appointments, and I sat in the bleachers at basketball games watching Erick play and Kaete cheer while curious observers asked, *"What's she going to do?"* and I sarcastically answered, *"Have a baby."* I sat quietly after answering. I realized my answer likely kept me at arm's length, on the other side of my brick wall, from someone who might truly care for and love Kaete and Erick in a way I didn't expect.

I began to change my responses. *"What do you mean?"*

This shift opened floodgates of loving kindness. Responses such as *Will she need childcare?* to *Will she want to graduate early?* flew around me in a non-judgmental way but with a curious wondering *How can we all help her be successful?* No one wanted her to be successful more than she, her dad, or I, but to consider that people whom she's known for most of her life also wanted the best for her was a new level of empathy I hadn't expected.

Game after game, I would see Erick's family members and not know what to say. Were they angry or scared? Were they truly excited or faking it to get through the moment? Did they have the same concerns I had, or was it just another bump in the road they were facing, with life moving forward as normal? Sometimes I wasn't sure and sometimes it was crystal clear.

Midway through the basketball season, I realized we would need insurance for the baby upon birth. Brian and I were looking into coverage possibilities. We were taking control of every ounce of care without considering Erick's parents and their interest in involvement with their grandchild.

During halftime of a game, I approached Sol, who was also at the game alone. We briefly chatted about insurance possibilities through misty eyes, and then he made a statement I can no longer remember. I only recall the tears filling his eyes and my strong desire to leave.

No. Not here. I can't do this in a gym full of people

who are watching to see how our families will navigate this.
I offered a short comment back and then, saved by the game restarting, returned to my seat in the crowd. Together we sat, separated by three rows of bleachers, yet all alone.

I sat behind him quietly, shaming myself for not being present for Sol as his emotions welled. I told myself that, as a counselor, I should have the ability to hold his concerns with empathy and kindness without walking away.

Those moments happened more frequently as time moved forward. With each one, I still believed I could be a source of strength for everyone... except me. It wouldn't occur to me until much later that I also needed kindness and to be gentle with myself. I couldn't hold him if I was unwilling to hold myself.

Just as with the doctor appointments, I would share these moments of awakening with Brian, he would apologize for not being able to be there, and for a tiny moment I felt we were together. Though he rarely left work early or participated in conversations regarding Kaete's pregnancy with anyone other than me, Sol, or Vivis, I never asked him to.

twelve | *Miracles*

There are two ways to live: as if nothing is a miracle, or as if everything is a miracle.   attributed to Albert Einstein

A 3D sonogram was scheduled on Erick's 15th birthday. The kids were on spring break, away from peers, and excited to get to know their little guy a bit more. They wanted to make sure he fit the name they had chosen and to provide Erick with the same feeling of excitement that Kaete could feel every day.

As we prepared to leave for the sonogram, Kaete asked if Erick could ride with us because his family was going to meet us there. Family? Based on past experience, I wondered what she meant by this. His mom, dad and brother? His aunts? When I asked

Erick who was going, he simply shrugged.

We drove the 30 minutes to the appointment chatting with each other and listening to Kaete excitedly ask questions about what her little baby would look like. To Erick, *"Do you think he'll have your nose?"* Without waiting for his response she looked to me, *"Mom, do you think you can see if he has hair?"* My response: *"I have no idea."*

When Brian and I were expecting our babies, we couldn't afford the extra sonogram. We spent our evenings and weekends envisioning what our surprise would look like. We talked with our parents, listened to them relive our birth stories, and pored over baby pictures, wondering what features each would inherit.

With our first, we were two young adults still in shock that we had a baby on the way. I hadn't experienced a menstrual cycle in more than a year, so finding out I was pregnant seemed like a trick God had played. While we always knew we wanted children, we could barely believe it when we learned one was on the way and I was already three months pregnant. Each appointment was an adventure, and

Brian attended every one with me. The sonogram was no different, with just the two of us together in a cold room.

Our first sonogram was exciting even though we couldn't see a thing. We wanted to know the gender so badly, but the little body had the cord stuffed between the legs, and legs crossed, securing anonymity for 20 more weeks. We knew nothing beyond the health and growth of our baby, and that turned out to be enough.

Our second sonogram was equally exciting, as we included 3½-year-old Jace. On the drive to the appointment, we asked if he wanted a brother or a sister. *"A brother!"* he shouted. *"I don't want a sister!"* as he scrunched his nose up at the thought.

In the hospital room he stood on a chair we had scooted up to the exam table, and joined us in anticipation as the sonographer showed him all the tiny baby parts on the fuzzy monitor. The legs, the arms, the beating heart, and the cutest little nose. Then she asked him, while looking at us, *"Do you want to know what it is?"* Our son replied, *"Is it a brother?!?!"* The woman's face made a small cringe as she looked at me and said, *"No... it's a sister!"* And, with that, our son's eyes widened as he jumped up and down on his chair and proclaimed, *"A sister?!? I always wanted a sister!!"*

The three of us laughed with relief to see him embrace exactly what was set before him. This exclamation of love and acceptance proved to be a true glimpse of who he would become as a brother. He became her best friend, protector, and model for handling all the hard stuff. They had conflicts, like the day he held her over the stair rail when she came into his room after he had asked her not to. But they also had each other's backs.

I shared the adorable Jace-and-the-sonogram story again, one Kaete had heard many times in her life, as we drove to her second sonogram appointment.

I recognized many cars as we pulled into the parking lot and remembered Kaete saying Erick's family was going to meet us there. She was right. Aunts, uncles, cousins, parents... everyone came to see this little life. We walked through the doors and were met with a wave of words and hugs. I felt distracted by the need to greet everyone out of politeness and fought to remain present for Kaete. A twinge of anxiety over sharing something so private with so many people, mixed with a hint of relief knowing we were going into a dark space, washed over my body as the assistant took us back to the tiny room with a large overhead video monitor and dimmed the lights.

The sonogram tech sat Kaete on a bed with Erick to her right, her dad to her left and me just over her left shoulder. Erick's family sat in the rows of chairs that had been brought in for the occasion. I joked that we should have brought snacks, and one of Erick's aunts asked if we were the largest group to cram into that tiny room. The sonographer counted us up and replied, *"Wow, 18! We've actually had 23 in here before."* The aunt seemed disappointed and asked with a chuckle, *"Were they Mexican, too?"* Everyone laughed and the tech responded with a smile, *"No. It was a miracle baby who was being celebrated while everyone was in town for the baby shower."*

As the tech began the crystal-clear video, I held on to the words *"miracle baby."* Wow! There he was. Perfect and beautiful, with his daddy's nose.

We left the sonogram to celebrate Erick's birthday as one big family. The gathering looked similar to the scene in *My Big Fat Greek Wedding* when Ian and his parents meet Toula's large Greek family. Only in our story, the Greeks were Mexican, and the wedding was a baby. *My Big Fat Mexican Baby* became the loving moniker I would think of when Brian and I attended Erick's family gatherings.

thirteen | *Celebrations*

Our deepest fear is not that we are inadequate. Our deepest fear is that we are powerful beyond measure. It is our light, not our darkness, that most frightens us.
Marianne Williamson

Kaete and Erick wrapped up their freshman year as the due date approached. Kaete was surrounded with love, as friends stopped by, bringing cold drinks, ice cream, and the excited chatter of teenage girls.

Our families celebrated the impending birth with baby showers. The first shower was hosted in our home and included all of her and Erick's aunts, cousins, and grandmothers. It was beautiful and sweet, marking the beginning of acceptance that so many family members were scared to offer and historically rejected. The energy was subdued, quiet, full of smiles and pleasantries. Kaete and baby received gifts handmade by neighbors, must-haves from cousins, and necessities from others.

A few weeks later, a family friend who had known Kaete all her life hosted the second shower. This friend was someone who had immediately picked me up for dinner the moment she heard Kaete was pregnant and held me as I cried and wondered about our future. She invited Kaete's closest friends and their mothers to share their favorite books and play a few games.

We were surrounded by precious gifts, including the attendance of my best friend who traveled from St. Louis with her daughters and a cradle made by the father of one of Kaete's best friends. This exhibition of love sent me into a state of tearful appreciation that ended the shower with a grand speech. Through tears and snot, I thanked the girls for being a source of love and support for Kaete, then turned to their mothers and thanked them for modeling what friendship and love look like. Kaete's eyes avoided mine the entire time, in an effort to flee my raw emotions.

We loaded the gifts in my car and drove home, laughing at the awkwardness of my impromptu speech, realizing as we pulled into the driveway we had one more shower to attend that evening. The house was already full of toys, books, clothes, and diapers. What else could they need?

Erick's family hosted the third and final shower. The invitation said it would begin at 5:30 p.m. Brian, Jace, Kaete, Erick, my friend, her daughters, and I decided to go early to help set up. When we arrived, we introduced everyone to Erick's family. They assured us there was nothing left to do to prepare. So, we all sat at a table and laughed and caught up, while Kaete and Erick greeted family members and friends as they arrived.

People arrived, and arrived. For two hours, friends and family continued to arrive, placing gifts in the corner of the event space. We began dinner, and people continued to arrive. We played games, and a few people continued to arrive while others left for other events. Throughout the evening the greatest celebration of life, full of food, games, laughter, and music, continued. Our family made a clean sweep, winning games against Erick's family. And Erick's family made a clean sweep in celebrating in a way that included everyone.

Around 9 p.m., the two exhausted soon-to-be-parents were encouraged to open gifts. The pile that had been built in the corner had to be deconstructed. For more than an hour, they opened gifts one by one as attendees looked on with joy and cheering. Erick read who each gift was from and pointed in their direction, often not sure who he was referring to. Sol and Vivis' friends and co-workers had showed up from all around to celebrate their journey to becoming abuelos.

Our table watched in awe of the love that surrounded this little family. The shower finished and our group laughingly acknowledged that our family and friends *do not* know how to party! When I look back at the pictures from that night, I continue to be filled with joy at the celebration that occurred.

fourteen | *Patients*

Maybe the journey isn't so much about becoming anything. Maybe it's about un-becoming everything that isn't really you, so you can be who you were meant to be in the first place. Paul Coelho

"I think my water broke."

Kaete stood on the front porch in the heat and humidity of the July evening. Her dad and I had taken our usual positions in our Adirondack chairs, facing west as the sun was setting. I glanced over, quickly noticing the puddle that had formed between her two bare feet, and responded with a laugh,

"I think you're right!"

We had waited so long for this moment. We made it through sports seasons, exams, vacations, and the completion of our son's freshman year of college. She had spent most of the summer staying inside, visiting with friends who stop by to chat, check on her, and bring her cold treats as her belly grew.

In the week leading up to this moment, we had hosted our former exchange student and his parents during their vacation in the States. Though the due date was still a week away, we all crossed our fingers for a birth during their visit.

We had hosted our student two years prior and loved him like one of our own. His parents were full of fun and energy that took them on bike rides around our community as their son showed him all the places he had hung out during his year in our home. We took difficult hikes with the goal of inducing a birth. We drove our son's 1978 Jeep CJ in hopes of bouncing a baby right out. Our neighborhood held its semi-annual block party, and still no baby.

Our exchange student and his family continued their vacation on through the Midwest before returning to Germany, promising to stop in again if the baby was born while they were stateside. And still no baby.

The heat of July raged as the due date came and went. Kaete was miserable, puffy, and sweaty most of the time. We hugged her often in hopes of getting a little kick from a tiny foot. We massaged her fluid-filled ankles in a game to see how long it would take before her skin returned to its plump smoothness. She asked Erick to rub her feet when she couldn't walk. She wanted to crawl into the cool water in a bikini and feel like a perky 15-year-old girl. Instead, she lay on the couch like a squishy water balloon on the verge of bursting.

As each day passed, she tried natural and alternative methods to induce labor: massage, acupuncture, essential oils, and long walks. So many long walks. Earlier in the day, she had thought her water broke so she, Erick, and I spent five hours at the hospital with her connected to monitors and innocently claiming labor wasn't "that bad" if this was it.

They sent us home when there were no signs of progression. Five days overdue, she was exhausted and feeling like the current situation was her permanent destiny. Though our brains knew it wasn't possible, Kaete, Erick, and I all silently wondered, *Will he ever get here?*

We returned home from the hospital. The two kids went inside to watch TV, Erick on the couch and Kaete bouncing relentlessly on the exercise ball. I joined Brian on the porch for a beer and shared the play-by-play of our day. Then, all at once, there she was. Huge smile, Erick also smiling by her side, both totally unaware of what was about to happen. We were ready and we were excited. The time to see how our lives would forever be changed had arrived.

Erick called his parents as we loaded up to drive to the tiny hospital 15 miles away.

We arrived at the same time as Sol and Vivis. Smiling and hugging and laughing all the way to the front door, as Kaete and Erick led the way. From behind, they looked like two young kids going on a chaperoned date with their parents, but as Kaete turned toward the hospital doors, her belly preceded her and she looked back at us as a mother.

One nurse checked Kaete in shortly after 9:00pm. Another staff member gave us parents (grandparents!) instructions and information on where we could relax, find a snack, or get food in their tiny town. All of this unfortunately useless so late in the evening, as nothing was open other than the gas station.

Kaete was directed toward the birthing suite we had visited months earlier, given a gown to change into, connected to monitors, and asked a series of questions about her labor progress. During this time, she had a few contractions, reminding everyone the moment was truly upon us as she confidently exclaimed, *"These aren't as bad as I expected!"* and *"That one was stronger! I can do this!"*

Kaete has always been aware of the strength in her body. Once, in middle school P.E., the teacher was encouraging his students to *"Give it all you got!"* as they ran "ladders." With one small glance from the teacher, Kaete knew she had to try harder to beat her previous time. Being a student who not only wanted to impress her teachers, but also prove to herself that she was strong, she gave her all. As the time ran out, so did Kaete. She left P.E. as her brain swirled and she became lightheaded while climbing three flights of stairs to her art class, where she promptly passed out.

In the delivery suite nurses and aides continued to ask Kaete questions, it became evident there was judgment on their faces and in their voices. One tone to Kaete and Erick sounded similar to a preschool teacher asking her students, *"Where should your hands be right now?"* Another, more monotone, voice to the grandparents was more like a museum curator who robotically gestures to an artifact while saying, *"...and on your right, you will notice..."* The small hospital had one other patient down the hall and only a handful of staff that night. All on duty were Mennonite women wearing simple dresses covered by medical smocks, and small bonnets covering what I have always assumed to be tightly wound buns of beautiful hair.

On the walls of the birthing suite were Bible verses and encouraging quotes about life. A small hand-stitched quilt hung over a comfortable recliner in the corner and a quilted pillow, also hand-stitched, was propped in the corner of a hospital-issued couch. Together our two families sat around and chatted as Kaete lay in bed, counting contractions, asking Erick for massage, ice chips, or to help her to get up and walk around.

The nurse they had met with for their initial tour and their birthing classes arrived and greeted everyone with a smile as she struck up a conversation with the soon-to-be parents. She went in and out of the room as needed, keeping everyone informed of labor progress, what to expect, and checking on Kaete and Erick's comfort.

She herself was a young mom who was six months pregnant with her third child. Full of energy and experience, she chatted comfortably with her patients, reminding them both how she could be reached if they needed anything: Kaete could use the call button, Erick could use the call button or come find her. She left the room again near midnight and turned to the anxious grandparent group, reminding us *"It could be a while"* and it might be best if we *"could all get a little rest."* We agreed to go to the lobby and sprawl out on the sofas and reclining chairs.

Leaving Kaete and Erick behind, I remembered a conversation with my friend whose son participated in the delivery of his daughter during his senior year of high school. As my friend recalled sitting in the waiting room with the girlfriend's parents, I had stopped her story and asked who all was in the delivery room. She calmly said, *"[Son] and [girlfriend]."*

In the days after our conversation, I cried and vowed that Kaete would not be in active labor without me by her side. Yet in the moment, I walked down the hall with Brian and our team mates, leaving our children behind to labor toward parenthood. I wasn't following the crowd, or avoiding out of exhaustion, but feeling pure peace.

In the hours leading up to our walk down this hall, I had watched Erick fetch ice chips, adjust pillows, and massage Kaete, responding to her every request. I had listened in as he asked her if there was anything she needed before he took his own break. I saw him stare at her and she at him while they whisper-talked as they had so many times in my living room. I gathered every bit of evidence that he was right where he needed to be when the nurse gave specific instructions on how to call her and he assured he would comply if Kaete needed her attention. He was right where he belonged and so was I.

In the lobby/waiting room, the four grandparents sat talking into the night – Brian on the couch to stretch out his long legs, Vivis, Sol, and I each taking a recliner.

We laughed as we shared childhood stories. Sol fixing bikes as a child to make some money. Vivis as his cute neighbor he always noticed but was too shy to talk to. They told the story of finding money on their honeymoon and how the little blessing allowed them to extend their vacation just a bit longer.

Brian and I described our high school romance, he the humble all-around athlete and me the busy cheerleader, dancer, anything-but-study, older girl. We laughed as we honestly shared that it could have been us in the same situation as Erick and Kaete, collectively realizing how God creates our path and we have no clear vision of the future no matter how much we believe or try to control situations.

A text from Kaete arriving around 3 a.m. – *"Can you come back here?"* – returned us all to the present. I leapt out of my reclined position, trying to hold in my excitement at being needed, while also feeling a tiny bit of loss that I might miss out on more storytelling leading to deeper understanding and relationship.

Entering the dim hospital room, I could see Kaete lying on her side facing the door, her face lit by the glow of the monitor. She was in pain as she looked at me. The nurse said Kaete was requesting an epidural. Due to her age, the hospital needed parental consent to administer any kind of anesthesia, but due to the situation, Kaete needed her own consent.

In the weeks leading up to her due date, Kaete was certain she wanted an unassisted delivery. Throughout her life, she had heard me share the stories of her and Jace's births, both without medication, though I would have taken anything if the timing had been right. During Jace's delivery, he became lodged in the birth canal and his heart rate dropped quickly. The doctor made the quick decision to use the vacuum extractor, ripping the cutest little cone-head straight from my body as I felt faint. Delivering Kaete, on the other hand, was incredibly quick. She arrived within two hours of my water breaking and two contractions after I was told I was too far along to receive an epidural. I would have loved the relief of an epidural yet always felt a sense of pride that my body forced me into childbirth without my consent.

Those were the stories she knew and wanted to emulate, yet after six hours of labor with very little sleep and nothing to eat, she needed to relax and allow her body to do what it had to do. She looked defeated as I asked her the questions we had practiced at home in case she begged for an epidural during labor. *"Where does it hurt? Do you really want one? Will you be able to relax if you have one?"* She answered, *"My back. Yes. Yes."* I asked the final question to Erick, *"Do you think she needs one?"* He nodded with a look of both relief and exhaustion. I gave the nurse the go-ahead to call in the anesthesiologist.

The doctor was tall and fit with sandy blond hair, appearing to be in his mid-30s. He entered the room and smiled at Kaete as he spoke to her quietly and softly with his hand on her shoulder. He was comforting and thorough in his explanation of what would occur and what he would need her to do. He encouraged her to relax and talked equally to both kids regarding the benefits and risks to both mother and child. *"Mother can relax and get some sleep, which allows her body to progress. Mother might have a headache as the medicine wears off."*

His voice trailed off as I stopped listening to the risks but instead focused on his comforting voice and kindness toward Kaete and Erick. He finished and explained to Kaete that only one person could be in the room with her as he administered the epidural, which meant she would have to decide between me and Erick. Beginning as she usually does when asked to make a decision, she said, *"I'm okay either way."* However, we all knew this was a decision we couldn't make for her, so we relaxed and watched her glance back and forth between me and Erick. With a sweet look toward Erick, Kaete settled on me. Erick left the room and we began the process of relieving her pain.

The doctor gave me instructions on how to help Kaete relax, to make certain she didn't move, and to help her breathe through contractions. As he attempted to sit her up, she experienced the wave of another agonizing contraction. Her face grimaced and her body turned back toward the bed, reaching for any position that would alleviate the pain, but the pressure was too much as she cried for it to stop.

My insides were overcome by the desire to protect her and to remove her from the situation, simultaneously filling with excitement at recognizing the end was coming closer and she would soon be holding her sweet boy. Between contractions, she sat up on the side of the bed as I knelt on the floor in front of her, holding both of her hands.

With her legs spread wide to provide enough space for her expanded belly to cradle between, I held her hands in mine as she hunched forward through another contraction. All the while the doctor encouraged her – *"You're doing great, keep breathing, we're almost there"* – between each step in his process, pausing only to allow the next wave of pain to pass.

As I knelt below her, I closed my eyes, took slow deep breaths, and began praying for this new little family. I prayed for Kaete's comfort, rest, and safety as she weathered through labor. I prayed for Erick's strength, encouragement, and courage as he supported her in the last few hours. I prayed for the doctors' protection and knowledge along our journey. And I prayed hard for their future to be filled with love, honor, joy, respect, anything that would bring the two of them closer to their own truth as they faced raising a family far earlier than any of their peers or family members ever had. The doctor finished and we both helped Kaete lie back down, hoping she would get comfortable enough to rest.

I left the room to rejoin my group in the lobby and found Erick standing just outside the delivery room door, waiting to return to Kaete's side. In collaboration, they waited for their lives to change.

Back in the lobby, I offered the play-by-play of epidural injection before each of us finally dozed off. A couple of hours later, the nurse arrived to wake us.

Kaete was close. It was time to call the physician and to prepare for delivery.

With sleepy smiles and excited chatter, we walked into the delivery room, rejoining our children, who looked rested and ready to face anything. Kaete was sitting up in bed. Erick stood at her right shoulder looking down on her with a smile. They both nodded and responded to each of us as we commented on the excitement we all felt. The nurse stood to the left of Kaete as each of us four grandparents settled around the room in separate chairs but close enough to hear and await the arrival of our grandson.

Dr. Annie arrived, dressed in her scrubs, strawberry-blonde ponytail trailing down her back. She greeted Kaete and Erick, chatting excitedly as she smiled at each grandparent around the room. Slowly and with detail, she explained to the kids what she was getting ready to do, what they could expect as each moment came upon them. Gentle and relaxed, yet noticeably excited, all four of them – Kaete, Erick, nurse, and doctor – slowly progressed toward the moment for Kaete to push.

Dilated to 10 centimeters, propped up in her bed with a clump of pillows behind her back, Kaete looked at all of us with a huge smile. Dr. Annie dropped the end of the bed to allow more space for the birth. Sol and Brian moved to a corner of the room that allowed them to be present and close by for their children, yet provided privacy for Kaete as she was exposed to deliver. The opposite held true for Vivis and I as we scooted our chairs closer to the end of the bed just over Dr. Annie's left side. I jokingly motioned that I was pretending to eat popcorn.

During our wait in the lobby, Brian and I had learned that Vivis had delivered all four of her boys via Caesarean section, thus never experiencing the length and exhaustion of labor in the same way Kaete was. Vivis felt so much appreciation and admiration that Kaete allowed her to be in the delivery room for this moment. She smiled, looking frequently at her baby boy, at Kaete, and at me as she waited to witness her grandson's arrival.

As Kaete pushed, the first glimpse of jet-black curly hair began to show. Vivis and I smiled at each other, gasping at the amount of hair on the top of the tiny head. More pushing offered more black hair, as Annie asked Erick if he wanted to watch his son arrive. Erick glanced at Kaete, and she gave him a nod of encouragement. He leaned toward her feet and glanced down just as the final push forced the pinkest round little body from her and into the world. One suction of the mouth and his sweet screams filled the room. Vivis and I had tears streaming down our faces as I looked across the room to see the two grandfathers' tear-streaked faces smiling back at us.

In one quick motion, he was cleaned up and offered to his momma to fall in love. Erick cut the cord, christening himself into parenthood. Grandparents stood close, hugging through the joy of this beautiful surprise.

July 16, 2016 at 10:03am: Theo Oliver entered the world to forever change how a community experiences parenthood.

fifteen | *Visitors*

The only way to make sense out of change is to plunge into it, move with it, and join the dance. Alan Watts

Theo was a popular patient in the tiny hospital away from our home. Friends of ours and members of both sides of our families were in and out the 24 hours following his birth. Holding, kissing, praying, taking selfies, and falling in love. The love that glued these two teenagers, their families, and their cultures together was contagious.

Though the visits were frequent and a bit overwhelming for my comfort, I had no way to prepare for what we would experience once we returned home. The friends and family members who had not visited the hospital converged on our lives once word got out that Theo had made his way home: cousins and their friends, friends who had not been interested in Kaete's pregnancy, friends who were overly involved in Kaete's pregnancy, friends and their parents, aunts, uncles, tias, tios, great-grandparents, abuelos, cousins, primos, neighbors, and friends' children. They were in and out, all day long.

At the end of the first day home, Brian and I gave Erick permission to go to Kaete's room to help her change Theo's diaper and clothes and get him to sleep. As far as Brian and I knew, this was Erick's first time to go up the stairs of our home and into our daughter's bedroom. The second story of our house was a designated safe boundary that Brian and I set in place in a rookie belief that we could protect our children from the unknown life-changing situation that would obviously occur if they had access to a bed and vulnerability in the comfort of a bedroom.

Walking into Kaete's room that night, I saw a new daddy cradling his baby on the edge of the bed while Kaete wearily put clothes and gifts on a chair to make space to nurse in bed. Suddenly I was hit with a wave of emotion, as I realized this young father was going to have to go home each night and leave Kaete to figure out sleeping, eating, changing, soothing, and bonding with their baby. Years of working with parents and teaching how to create healthy attachment and bonding with their children stirred an internal conflict I couldn't shake. It didn't make sense that Erick would be left out of so much when any other parent, in any other situation, would be side-by-side with their partner to figure it out together, as a team.

I turned to Brian and quietly said, *"I think he should stay."*

I wasn't surprised to hear the love of my life respond with, *"Me, too."*

With no previous discussion or planning, we turned to Erick and I said, *"Would you like to stay here?"*

His eyes met mine and, with a smile, he nodded. I encouraged him to call his mother for permission that she quickly granted. That night, sleeping in the same room, the three of them began their journey toward becoming a family. Kaete and Erick woke together to feed, change, and soothe Theo as he grew.

sixteen | *Translations*

Let love be the foundation. Whether or not there is friendship, whether or not there is agreement or understanding, let there be love.

For the next three years, Erick lived with us while trying to find balance between the family he created and the family he was born into. I felt the pain of Vivis losing her boy to our home, just as I had felt I was losing Kaete to their family during pregnancy. I encouraged Kaete to spend more time at Erick's house to build bonds. The first few weekends, they slept at Erick's house, but learned that switching from bed to bed and house to house was too inconsistent for Theo and made it too difficult for Kaete to relax enough to nurse.

School started as Vivis and I took turns caring for Theo during the day while Kaete and Erick went to school. Each month I would share my work schedule, and Vivis would adapt her schedule to fit. We created our own gesture-filled language to explain what Theo needed or his latest trick as we transferred him between families. We laughed and celebrated when we successfully understood what the other was saying. One time, when we were taking way too long to interpret "banana," Theo watched from his car seat, curiously glancing between his Nana and Abuelita, as our gestures grew more dramatic and our laughter became louder. With celebration in our understanding we hugged as we glanced over to see Theo clapping and kicking in pride for both of us.

Kaete and Erick excelled at parenting. They took Theo everywhere they could and spent every moment making decisions that were in his best interest. They lit up when they arrived home and received their baby back from his Nana or Abuelita. They found support in the local Parents as Teachers program, and they attended school functions with Theo in tow.

Brian and I, however, were never clear on our role of raising these two teenage parents. Were we parenting Erick, or was he simply a guest? I fought to find my groove parenting Kaete while she parented... and I really never felt successful learning how to live with a young couple who had very little relationship experience, and were surrounded by drama every day in high school. We each had to fight our way through finding respectful boundaries when we had no clear idea of what boundaries would be needed.

It was painful to live with Kaete and Erick when they disagreed without wanting to jump in. I crossed the line many times and apologized just as many.

One night, after a big conflict led him to say hurtful words, and her to begin the process so many young women fall into, of believing what he said was true, I stepped in to offer what I considered healthy boundaries. I walked into her room, where they were fighting, Theo asleep on the bed, them standing on each side facing each other. I sat on the edge of her dresser and began teaching them how to treat someone you love.

I looked at Erick first. *"If you truly believe she is what you called her, then why in the world would you want to be with someone you think so little of?"*

What I was keeping myself from saying was, *Get out! Get out now and do not come back!*

I turned to Kaete, with a slow deep breath, and said, *"And if you respect yourself, why in the world would you want to be with someone who thinks so little of you?"*

What I was keeping to myself was, *Run for the hills and don't look back! This is NOT what love is!*

As I sat, I looked back and forth at each of them, as they glanced up at me.

I finished what I had to say with *"I honestly don't know what to do."*

Looking at Erick, I said, *"If it weren't for Theo, I would ask Kaete to break up with you right now. She doesn't deserve this and neither do you. But you have someone else to think about. Someone who is watching you to learn how to love."*

To both of them, I said, *"I hope you can figure this relationship out without calling each other names or being hurtful."*

I hopped down from my perch and walked out as I realized, *This is* exactly *what love is.* Love is the sharp moments where you wish you could take back hurtful words and behaviors. Love is not feeling gushy all the time but instead choosing to stay in a relationship and fight for it when it's worth fighting for. But love is also recognizing when that relationship has expired and it is time to respectfully grow beyond. I angrily prayed to God that those two kids would figure out which direction they were headed before their anger and passive aggressiveness began to affect Theo.

I sent Brian a text, begging him to bring me something home from his trip to Colorado with Jace. *Something* from Colorado would surely take the edge off.

I would never know the relief of an edge being taken off in such a way, but I would continue to come face to face with teenage drama, family boundaries, and the desire to run far, far away in an effort to create space but also to avoid controlling two lives that I wanted, and sometimes felt as if I needed, to control.

seventeen | *Endings & Beginnings*

Just because I carry it all so well doesn't mean it's not heavy.
Author unknown

Through three years of high school as parents, grandparents, and teammates, we all stuck to our original goal of giving two young parents the space they needed to be adolescents with a sidekick. Erick continued to play football, golf, and another year of basketball. Kaete was involved in all the extra-curricular activities that interested her, ultimately becoming a content editor for the school news-magazine and being inducted into the Spanish, Quill & Scroll, and National Honor Societies. Both achieved certificates as a springboard into their projected futures in emergency and pediatric medicine.

In the months leading up to graduation, I expected banquets and parties. I expected to drink more wine and sit quietly in an effort to slow down the pace of the moment and savor every second. I didn't expect the array of award ceremonies and the last-minute details of hosting a graduation party for someone who had an opinion.

When Jace had graduated four years earlier, the majority of his awards and recognition banquets came during his final swim season. He spent the last few months of his senior year playing video games, hanging out with friends, and going through college portfolios to decide the best fit for him. When it came to his party, he knew who he wanted to have it with and the two of them sat back while the two mothers planned. Technically, I watched the other mom make beautiful plans while I wrote checks and arrived early to set up.

This time around, I spent more time traveling for work and hoping for the best, as I rearranged my calendar to attend scholarship competitions, achievement award ceremonies, homecoming crowning, and honor banquets.

I sat back in amazement at what occurred around me. The scholarship competition that began with 600 participants narrowed down week after week until there was a winner. Kaete made it through two rounds and received a hefty award to one of the two schools she had chosen in her next step toward becoming a physician assistant.

Award ceremonies swelled with appreciation for hard work and a job well done by Kaete and her peers. They had spent hours applying for and competing for local, state, and national scholarships and in a matter of 45 minutes knew who had received which.

Induction ceremonies signified consistency in academics and provided a visual representation of those achievements with a tassel, pin, or cord. Activity banquets recognized competitive achievements and completion of an academic career in the activity was being recognized. Each time I sat quiet and still, not knowing what the achievement actually meant until a single moment when I lost my breath in pride.

I was proud when an entire student section burst into loud applause at the mention of Theo's name on homecoming night. I was proud when Kaete's journalism adviser explained her state ranking and the level of competition she was up against. Those moments proved how hard she had pushed herself to meet all the same goals she had before she knew she'd be a young mother. It solidified in me how much effort it took to plan and coordinate schedules to fit in activities, homework, jobs, sports, and dating. It reminded me how hard some days were when I felt angry from trying to balance parenting her while she parented Theo. All these moments were a celebration of the beauty and the courage it took to keep forging ahead through challenges.

All the while, Theo attended everything: football games and hanging out with the guys, homecoming and crafting with the girls. Awards ceremonies, proms, senior nights, banquets, and celebrations swirled around this tiny family from the first baby shower to the last graduation party. It doesn't feel like we ever found a groove, or that things were ever going as smoothly as expected.

As I remember all the sweet moments, I barely see the hard ones. The anger in the front yard when neither Kaete nor I was willing to hear the other's point of view. The pain from grief or fear over the unknown. Or the times when I wanted to rescue her, wishing I could change the outcome to make her life easier. I know those moments were there, because that was when we simultaneously grew. Those moments gave us power to heal and find new ways to communicate. They gave us pause to reflect and focus on what we individually wanted as well as what we desired in our relationship with each other, and to make changes to line up with our dreams.

Today, Kaete and Erick are homeowners, working toward their future, while thrust into the world of "parents" instead of "teen parents."

epilogue | *Listening In*

Find out who you are and be that person. That's what your soul was put on this earth to be. Find that truth, live that truth and everything else will come. Ellen DeGeneres

In my profession, I've had opportunities to speak and train others in parenting, attachment, mental health, empathy, and self-compassion. I worked in private practice with parents whose children had been removed from their care due to neglect and abuse. I sat in my office listening to parents who wanted to "get it right" or to "do better than was done to me." Sometimes the parents were addicts whose pain was so deep they couldn't provide safe care for their children. Sometimes the parents experienced anxiety so acutely they needed their children to behave a certain way in order to feel safe enough to function. And sometimes they were parents who were doing exactly what was done to them and they couldn't understand what was so wrong.

I grew up in a family where parents raised their voice, siblings fought, and spankings were regular responses to misbehavior. I remember walking away from conflict to the barn loft or abandoned chicken coop where I could create a fantasy world of parenting. Pretending I was the mommy, I would practice listening to my imaginary children's experiences (often inviting my younger siblings to play a role in my dramatic interpretation) and responding in the way I wanted to be responded to.

My parents were loving and protective and raised four children with wildly different personalities and behaviors. Though they parented equally, it was far from fair. A glance of disapproval could shred my heart, whereas my older brother would argue for why his "misbehavior" should be allowed.

I suppose it was in those moments of fantasy parenting and reflection that I became a counselor of sorts – first to myself and my siblings, then to my friends, and later to families in crisis. Frequently I was told I had a "knack for it" and I was "good at it," but inside I felt like a fraud. How they could believe in me when I knew that sometimes I was daydreaming as they were talking? Or that I often prayed for cancellations so I could have a small moment of peace in a stressful world?

I held the belief that if I was really good at my job, I could heal everyone who came through my door. Repeatedly in my own therapy and through clinical supervision, I was told I couldn't save everyone, or that no one changes until they are ready. But I wanted to. I wanted everyone to feel free of their traumas, illnesses, and pain. Except for me. I was severely afflicted with perfection.

Fighting the need to be perfect was painful and lonely. It was a place that created undue pressure on me to save people from themselves and from their own growth through processing and letting go. It built a wall so high that no one could climb, tear down, or penetrate it, that kept out love and freedom.

My addiction to perfection was exposed the moment I learned of Kaete's pregnancy, and every moment that followed, as I came face to face with my inability to protect Kaete from the hurt, pain, and judgment that is routinely bestowed upon our teen parent population. I fought judgment of myself and learned to embrace forgiveness. I felt the shame of sharing stories with my children from jobs where I actively worked to reduce the number of teen pregnancies. I rewrote my belief system to fight for respect for young parents instead of putting them in the same research projects as our addicted, homeless, or student drop-out populations. I participated in conference calls, actively listening to a topic I disagreed with. I tried to hold everyone up around me while they wrapped their brains around how these two innocent babies were going to be parents. Every single thing I fought for professionally, I second-guessed, and everything I was currently fighting for, I loved.

The counselor in me wanted to sit with Sol and

Vivis and help them process whatever they were feeling, but my own emotions sent me running in the opposite direction, or caused me to make a joke to avoid those emotions. The attachment specialist in me wanted to teach Kaete and Erick every single thing about growing a healthy baby and creating healthy attachment while simultaneously shielding my own baby from every glance, pain, or judgment. Ironically, attachment is created in moments of distress and the caregiver's response to the child's distress predicts the outcome and strength of the attachment (Bowlby, 1988). The trainer in me wanted to scream out to everyone I saw and worked with, *"LOVE THEM!,"* as they served children and families while raising their own. Sometimes I would make light of a situation that felt like a load of bricks on my chest.

Recently, I encountered two women, at the same conference, who successfully tore down my brick wall as they shared their reflections of me. After my first presentation of the day, I was happy to see a familiar teacher approach me. She had attended many of my trainings in years past and it felt good to have her there. After we hugged, she pulled back and, with her Southern accent, said, *"You've changed. Maybe it's me. But I'm pretty sure it is you."*

Tears filled my eyes, and I believed her. I've changed.

Before the beginning of my second session another participant approached me to say, *"I've followed your Facebook page for a while and was amazed at how you responded to your daughter's pregnancy... My daughter just announced she is pregnant and I never would have responded the way I did without your words [to guide me]."*

More tears, as these reflections showed me that work and growth are available, and were quite possible.

As I sit with the words of these two women today, I think of all of the stories and questions asked over the course of Kaete and Erick's journey. I learned that when we are witnessing someone survive and be shaped by a situation, quite possibly a situation we can't imagine ourselves in, we perk up and listen in hopes we can be just as strong.

As with so many stories, there is no one who can identify fully with what I experienced. There were many ways I actively fought against what was right in front of me. I overworked. I complained. I felt resentment. I also adapted and fought for exactly what I believed was true. I observed. I loved. I supported.

None of these are mutually exclusive. I don't believe I could have felt free enough to observe if I hadn't been fueled to grow beyond resentment. I don't believe I could have felt exhausted enough to complain if I wasn't fully supportive. And I certainly don't believe I would have loved the same if I did not have the opportunity to step away through work and return in love.

I tried dissociating my way through events in order to not take on anyone's energy of judgment, pity, or interest. It never worked. I left get-togethers and sporting events feeling exhausted. Sometimes I was overzealous and sometimes I was quietly guarded, always prepared to protect my heart, Kaete's privacy, and Theo's life.

Many times, I shared too much. Sometimes I didn't share a thing. I had friends who were supportive and others who corrected. Some stood close by and others faded off. Family was a weird paradox of knowing exactly what they thought about teen pregnancy based on my experience as a sexually active teen, while simultaneously watching them wrap Kaete's little family in love and acceptance, especially the family member who entered our home during the pregnancy.

Figuring out how to maintain healthy boundaries and advocate for Kaete's parenting was the most difficult task. As her mom, I felt a calling to teach her how to stand up for what was important to her, and if that didn't work, to ask her father and me for support. Societal and cultural norms suggest a teen parent doesn't know what s/he is doing. Stepping in to correct, rescue, or lecture is how adults commonly respond to young parents, but it's not what is needed.

Of course, with the blending of two families, there is stress, which offered many opportunities to support our daughter. I prefer to walk right toward conflict while Brian calmly listens and understands each side. Together we found ourselves sitting across from Sol and Vivis, searching to find respectful clarity between Kaete's needs and their family's hopes. Most of the time, we were successful, and sometimes we walked away feeling we made things worse.

I chose a path of "listening in" that worked for me. I stepped back from the spaces that distracted me (church, boards, committees, and private practice) and embraced practices of reflective pause (meditation, writing, nature, and fitness).

There were so many moments I felt breathless from the load I carried. When I share those experiences with Brian, he reflects and describes the feeling of butterflies in his chest, each time pointing to the same location where I felt the bricks. Over our hearts.

acknowledgments | *Dream Teams*

My book team:

To my coach, Dallas Woodburn: You taught me how to create and share my story with more courage than I knew was possible. Your honest and encouraging approach challenged me to dive deeper than I would have done alone.

My cheerleader, Angela Thompson: On my roughest days, I heard you say that my work is important. I am eternally grateful for your loving nudges.

The sideline support: Erika Lopez, Kelsey Donini, Cathy Lancelotta, Bibi Herran, Jenny Spencer, and Melissa Posten, for reading and re-reading until my words became clear.

Craig Doan, thank you for sharing your story, for getting Jace on the water, and for giving me a male perspective as you cleaned up my content. Dear, Jennifer Chappell Deckert, your vision and history of this story allowed this book to bloom. My editor, Melanie Zuercher, you fine-tuned and clarified my voice to make this book shine.

My community team:

Big thanks to the ladies who found me and stood close during school events: Diana Kuhn, Michelle Bergquist, and Renee Hamm. Your chatter, distractions, and ability to sit with me did not go unnoticed. Keri Mick, you grabbed me and took me aside to see me and my girl before I could see clearly. I've always loved that about you. Office space and book study gals, Debbie Robinson, Marlene Ewert, Jen Chappell Deckert, Kim Stahly, Joanna Bjerum, Joy Hoofer, Carrie Holler, and Sharon Schmidt, you didn't know what you were getting into, yet you showed up time after time.

Sarah Whillock, thank you for supporting Kaete, Erick & Theo during those first three years.

They learned so much from you.

My heart team:

Kim Stahly, Jennifer Vogts, Jana Hinz, Alicia Gregov, and Heather Ochoa, your ability to listen and love without judgment set me free.

Stahlys, Warkentines, Hoofers, and Lowes, your friendship provided more comic relief and fresh perspective than Brian and I could have wished for.

Becky Bailey, thank you for sharing your wisdom that directed me down a path of acceptance.

The medical team:

Dr. Annie Fast, Tami Werner, Kim, Jodi, and the staff at Partners in Family Care, watching you love and respect Kaete, Erick, and Theo opened my eyes to a new version of community.

Angie Schmidt, Lynnette Hendrickson, and James Jerde, thank you for providing every safe option to provide Kaete comfort in the days overdue.

The school team:

Big thanks to the staff of NHS! It was inspiring

to watch each of you wrap Kaete and Erick in support. Melinda Rangel, Molly Schauf, and Scott Seirer, thank you for fighting for childcare for our teen parent population. We didn't achieve our goal, but we raised a lot of awareness. Jana Crittenden and Lisa Moore, what a gift you both are as you each take time to continually direct students toward their dreams.

The family team:

My momma and daddy, Penny Ewert and Bill Horton, for standing solid and showing love. Leon and Janet Schmidt, for always offering grace no matter what.

Sol and Vivis, thank you for raising an amazing young man and for loving Kaete as your own. You complete our team and we are forever grateful.

Jace Schmidt, you are my heart and my eyes. Your ability to see and relate never ceases to amaze me. Thank you for taking so many hours to edit and design my book. Major gratitude for building my website and helping me look sharp.

Kaete and Erick, where do I begin? You

freaked me out, and then quickly reminded me who you are: kind, loving, honest, committed, human, dedicated, hard-working, and loyal. Theo is the luckiest kid with you as his parents.

My soul and my soft side, Brian: You are exactly what I need during every minute of every day. I can't thank you enough for loving me through every wild idea and thought I have. This book happened because you believed in me.

notes | *Quotes*

<u>one</u>: Quote by L.R. Knost. I love her work and her freedom to parent from a different perspective than the one in which she was raised. www.littleheartsbooks.com

<u>two</u>: Quote by Joanna Gaines from *The Magnolia Journal,* Spring 2019.

<u>three</u>: Quote by Eckhart Tolle from *Oneness with All Life* (Penguin Books, 2009).

<u>four</u>: Quote by Becky Bailey, Ph.D., from *Creating the School Family* (Loving Guidance Inc., 2011).
On page 31, Becky was the trainer I refer to when

asking how to protect Kaete. Her words became something I would return to when I felt like I was losing emotional control. I also took them too far on many occasions as I shut down parts of me that could have offered more support to Kaete.

<u>five</u>: Quote by Dan Millman from *Way of the Peaceful Warrior* (HJ Kramer, 2006).

<u>six</u>: Quote by Benjamin Mee, as played by Matt Damon, in *We Bought A Zoo* (20th-Century Fox, 2011). I love this quote. It is one I say to myself often when faced with something new or vulnerable. I've learned that it really does only take 20 seconds of insane courage to do just about anything.

<u>seven</u>: Quote by Aniesa Hanson.
www.aniesahanson.com

<u>eight</u>: Quote by Tamara Levitt, author and narrator for Calm.com. The Calm app has provided me with daily opportunities to relax and reflect, ultimately guiding me toward more clarity when I listen in.

<u>nine</u>: Quote by Henry David Thoreau from his personal journal, August 5, 1851.

<u>ten</u>: Quote by Thich Nhat Hanh from *Being Peace* (Parallax Press, 1987).

<u>eleven</u>: Quote by Anne Lamott from *Plan B: Further Thoughts on Faith* (Riverhead Books, 2004). Anne is my favorite author. I hope she reads my book.

<u>twelve</u>: Quote by Albert Einstein, maybe. When I searched for the origin of this quote, I fell down a rabbit hole of information on whether Einstein would say such a thing. Maybe he did, maybe he didn't. I like it.

<u>thirteen</u>: Quote by Marianne Williamson from *A Return to Love: Reflections on the Principles of a Course in Miracles* (Harper One, 1996).

<u>fourteen</u>: Quote by Paul Coelho from *The Alchemist* (Harper One, reprint 2014). If you haven't read *The*

Alchemist, you must pick it up as soon as you put this book down.

fifteen: Quote by Alan Watts, philosopher and writer of more than 20 books.

sixteen: Quote on Calm.com, on International Day of Peace, Sept. 21, 2018. This app is life-changing, I tell you!

seventeen: Quote from www.wordporn.com, author unknown.

epilogue: Quote by Ellen DeGeneres on Instagram.

Bowlby, John. *A Secure Base: Parent-Child Attachment and Healthy Human Development*. Basic Books, 1988.

about the author | *Shana*

Shana Lynn Schmidt is a licensed counselor, parenting coach, infant & early childhood mental health specialist, Conscious Discipline® Certified Instructor, writer, and Nana. She lives in a small Kansas town with her husband Brian, not far from where they grew up, with their two dogs and an empty nest.